AMERICAN SIGN LANGUAGE FOR KIDS

101 Easy Signs for Nonverbal Communication

American Sign Language for Kids

ROCHELLE BARLOW

Includes Tips for Children with ASD

ILLUSTRATIONS BY
NATALIA SANABRIA

callisto
publishing
an imprint of Sourcebooks

Copyright © 2019 by Callisto Publishing LLC

Cover and internal design © 2019 by Callisto Publishing LLC

Illustrations: 2019 © Natalia Sanabria; 2019 © Chloé Besson, pages 150-154; © Shutterstock, pages 148-149

Author Photo: courtesy of Rochelle Barlow.

Art Director: Emma Hall

Art Producer: Sue Smith

Editor: Justin Hartung

Production Editor: Gleni Bartels

Published by Callisto Publishing LLC C/O Sourcebooks LLC

P.O. Box 4410, Naperville, Illinois 60567-4410

(630) 961-3900

callistopublishing.com

This product conforms to all applicable CPSC and CPSIA standards.

Source of Production: Wing King Tong Paper Products Co.Ltd. Shenzhen, Guangdong Province, China

Date of Production: September 2023

Run Number: 5034921

Printed and bound in China.

WKT 3

To Carol, my loving Grandmama, who first introduced me to ASL.
I hope I live my life as you lived yours.

CONTENTS

6 Playtime 105

7 Everyday Conversation 121

8 Alphabet and Numbers 147

INTRODUCTION

PEOPLE OFTEN ask me why I learned American Sign Language (ASL) and when I started. Most people assume I began to learn because I knew someone who was Deaf or because I had a Deaf family member. My story is unique, and fitting for this book.

My Grandmama loved to read books to her grandchildren. Her bookcases were filled with the best books, and she spent a lot of time with each of us reading our favorite books. No matter how many books I could choose from, I always chose the same one, *Koko's Kitten*, by Francine Patterson.

Koko's Kitten is the story of Koko, the gorilla who learned sign language. As a kid, I loved monkeys and gorillas; add in a new language that fascinated me, and I was hooked. So began my journey, at a very young age. I began to learn ASL when I was six years old. My mother bought me an ASL dictionary, and for years I learned as much as I could on my own. I went to a private tutor and eventually took classes in high school and college. I began interpreting for a Deaf friend when I was 17 years old. When I was in college for Deaf education, I began to teach my friends and tutor fellow classmates. As an adult, my experience and signing took off. I have interpreted as a career for 15 years in a number of settings, and my favorite places are schools. I started teaching individuals and then went into families' homes to teach Deaf children, those who were hard of hearing, and children who had autism or Down syndrome. Six years ago I began to teach online in order to reach more people and help more families and individuals.

I am passionate about getting sign language into homes and communities to provide more access and greater opportunities for children who are Deaf or hard of hearing or who otherwise struggle to communicate.

This book will help your entire family have meaningful communication with one another. You will discover how easy and enjoyable it is to learn sign language. The overwhelming questions—and the worry of "where do I start?"—will fade, and you'll gain confidence each time you pick up this book and work together to sign.

It is of the utmost importance that you learn ASL alongside your child. You'll find a whole new world opened up to you in the Deaf community. The Deaf community welcomes all who sign, not just those who identify as Deaf, and is extremely supportive and passionate about Deaf culture. You and your family will appreciate the opportunity to connect with a like-minded community, and your support system and friendships will double.

Who Is This Book For?

American Sign Language for Kids provides the easiest, most effective method for teaching ASL to your child and your entire family. It's written for parents, grandparents, caregivers, and teachers of children ages 3 to 6.

The aim of this book is to help children diagnosed with hearing loss learn and practice communication tools and to teach their families how to communicate with them. It is also intended for nonverbal children or those with limited speech abilities due to autism spectrum disorder (ASD) or other developmental disorders, such as Down syndrome. Finally, this book will help hearing children communicate with Deaf or nonverbal family members, and hearing children will also benefit from the improved vocabulary and spelling skills that ASL can provide.

This book will teach you 101 signs and provide practice activities, valuable tips, and additional resources. The chapters have been organized to help children communicate their most vital needs. Armed with these signs and activities, you and your child can hit the ground running, reducing the stress that children face when they struggle to express themselves.

This book is not a substitute for in-person ASL education for Deaf and hard of hearing children and families. Instead, it is a resource, a guide, and in some cases, a refresher.

Similarly, this book is not a replacement for behavioral resources for kids diagnosed with ASD or other developmental disorders; instead, it provides a way to help you and your child communicate more easily. It is a tool for you, your family members, and fellow caregivers to use and enjoy so you can work together as a team.

How to Use This Book

Before you jump into learning the signs, take a moment to understand how this book is organized and how best to navigate it for maximum success and ease of use.

In chapter 1, we cover all the essentials you need to know to get started learning ASL. We discuss how it fits into your home life and answer questions and concerns you may have.

Then we begin with the first 10 signs you'll want to know right away. These signs cover the most important needs and include the most common words you will use with your child. After that, we move into categories of signs that are the most frequently used by young children, including family and feelings, meal-time, home, playtime, and everyday conversation. While these chapters have been arranged in order of relative importance, you can approach them in the order that best fits your and your family's needs.

Throughout the chapters, we cover various aspects of sign language that aren't expressed with your hands. These components of ASL include facial expressions and nonmanual markers and are shown with the face, head, and body. These are integral to clear signing.

The last chapter covers the ASL alphabet and the numbers. Numbers in ASL are not signed like the traditional counting on your fingers you did as a child. Most of the signs you will learn use a variation of handshapes found in the ASL letters and numbers. The most common are **A, O, S, 1,** and **5.** Although you can learn the letters and numbers at any point, you may find it helpful to learn them earlier on to better understand what your hands should look like when forming the various signs you will learn. I suggest that you, the adult, learn the alphabet and numbers first, before learning the signs. Wait to teach your child the alphabet and numbers until you've worked through the majority of the book or until you reach chapter 8.

Each sign in this book has an accompanying description to help you better understand the illustration of the sign. This will help you know that you are signing each one correctly. You will also find a memory tip for each sign, along with tips about similar signs or other meanings for the sign, teaching tips, and more. At the end of each chapter, there are practice activities to bring together the signs you've learned in that chapter. As you progress through the book, the activities will combine the signs from multiple chapters to further challenge you and to increase your ability to fully use the signs.

Learn the signs yourself before you introduce and teach them to your child. Your child may enjoy looking at the illustrations with you, but to best help them form the signs and for you to be able to make corrections, you'll need to know the sign first.

1

ASL Basics

IN THIS CHAPTER, we'll cover what ASL is, discuss the benefits for your child and your family, and explore accessible ways to introduce your child to sign language. You'll also learn the basic rules of etiquette when interacting within the Deaf community.

Each child and family learns and grows at their own rate. We'll discuss what you can expect for your child and yourself.

As I'll remind you throughout this book, be patient and loving with yourself. Take your time to master the signs, and focus on enjoying the process. This is much more important than speed.

At times you may feel anxious and behind, but I promise you, it will come and you *can* sign. You will be able to communicate with your child faster than you imagine. Commit to showing up, and you'll see consistent progress.

What Is American Sign Language?

American Sign Language is a beautiful and powerful language full of expression. There are some important things to know about the three types of signed languages you'll see in the United States and much of Canada, which are Signed Exact English (SEE), Pidgin Sign English (PSE), and American Sign Language (ASL).

These first two variations of sign language were created by those in the hearing community and are not true languages:

SEE is English word for word, sound for sound, with your hands. For instance, in SEE you would sign each syllable in "I am go-ing to the store," in that order. The majority of signs are initialized, meaning they start with the first letter of the word being signed, such as G for *go*. It can be quite cumbersome and hard to understand and is not widely accepted within the Deaf community since SEE is not the language of the community.

PSE is a hybrid of SEE and ASL. PSE falls on a spectrum from SEE to ASL, depending on the frequency of use of initialized signs and the structure of sentences. If the grammar leans toward English syntax, then you are on the SEE end of the spectrum.

ASL is the preferred language of the Deaf community. It is the fourth most used language in the United States, with roughly half a million to 2 million speakers—and this number does not include those who know ASL but do not use it as their primary language. Americans have been using ASL since the early 1800s, and language experts recognized it as a true language in 1960.

ASL is a visual language based on specific hand gestures and their placement relative to the body, along with head and body movements, mouth morphemes (the specific shapes your mouth makes to add meaning to a sign), facial expressions, and other nonmanual markers. ASL is expressed with your hands, body, and face, and it is received with the eyes.

ASL is a powerful, evolving language, with as much information expressed as in any oral language. It is expressive and robust, and will give you and your child full access to language and communication.

How It Can Help Your Child

Learning American Sign Language as a family will be the adventure of a lifetime. I wish I could personally look you in the eyes, sit down with you, and help you fully understand the gift you're giving yourself, your child, and your entire family by learning ASL.

Your desire to communicate with your child, and to give them the gift of language, is an uncommon reward for children with hearing loss or developmental disabilities, and I don't say that lightly. I applaud your choice. Your child will one day thank you.

Your family will become a stronger, more solid unit. You will discover and learn together. You'll make mistakes and help one another. ASL will benefit each member of your family, whether they need to use it or not. Career opportunities can open up for a person who is bilingual in English and ASL.

CHILDREN WITH HEARING LOSS

Your child may or may not have a hearing aid or cochlear implant. As you will soon find out, hearing aids don't always work, and sometimes they break, especially if your child is very young. There are circumstances when wearing them is not possible, such as while swimming or playing sports. Sweat can interfere with the mechanism, batteries can die, and kids can jump into the pool without first removing the device. If their hearing aid were to go out during class, what would your child do? Hearing loss can also worsen over time.

It's important that your child has multiple ways to communicate in a variety of circumstances. Even if you're sending your child to a hearing school, and raising them with speech and lip reading, both of you knowing ASL will guarantee that they are never without information. Even in the best of circumstances, lip reading isn't a foolproof method. Relying on lip reading for your child's education would be as if you put headphones on a hearing student that allowed them to hear only every sixth word in a class lecture and didn't fill them in on what they missed. It would be a miracle if they learned much at all.

Sign language can open previously closed doors by providing more opportunities for communication and information access.

CHILDREN WITH ASD

If I could wish something into existence, it would be more families using ASL with their children on the autism spectrum. Sign language can give your child a voice to express themselves when they can't do it verbally. It can help them share ideas and understand what's going on around them. It is highly successful in helping them become verbal and be more accepting of physical prompts and in teaching them to imitate.

HEARING CHILDREN WITH DEAF FAMILY MEMBERS

Being able to communicate with every family member is important. Sign language can build connections within families with mixed hearing and developmental abilities.

For all children, sign language can help with their spelling, confidence, and ability to express themselves.

How to Introduce Your Child to ASL

Introducing your child to ASL will be an easy and fun conversation. They'll be so excited and relieved to have a way to communicate with you that they'll be eager to get started. If you approach this conversation with joy and enthusiasm, they will feel it from you as a positive thing. ASL is a gift for your little one and your family; embrace it, and they will, as well.

When you introduce sign language to your child, keep their needs in mind. Consider whether it might be better suited as a family activity with everyone involved or as a private conversation. Your child's level of comprehension, communication ability, and age may also be factors to consider. If they're not ready for a discussion, save it for another time.

When your child is ready for a conversation about sign language, or if they ask you questions about it, approach it with a spirit of adventure and opportunity. You can discuss things such as:

- What ASL is
- Why you decided to learn ASL
- How ASL will help them in the future
- The reasons you're excited about using ASL together (make a list)

The first time you introduce sign language, make it a family night. Check the Resources (page 157) to find wonderful storybooks and DVDs you can read and watch as a family. Find one you think your child would enjoy.

Afterward, you can learn one or two signs from the story or begin to learn signs from chapter 2, "The First 10 Signs."

If your child has a favorite animal, food, or special toy, find the sign in this book and learn it together as your first sign. They will love being able to talk about one of their favorite things.

The Family That Signs Together . . .

The most important reason to learn and teach ASL is your child's welfare. I touched on this earlier, but it bears mentioning again. Your child will feel included as a member of the family rather than like a lonely outsider. I cannot emphasize the importance of this enough. You are already making great strides to help your child feel loved and that they have every advantage. I commend you.

Unfortunately, many in your position do not take the time and effort to learn and use sign language with their child, leaving them alienated from the world without much language or ability to communicate. The devastation that leaves runs deep. There are many Deaf and hard of hearing people who have no connection with their family or haven't spoken to them in years. Many hold deep pain about the isolation they felt among their family, in their own home.

Signing might feel impossible for some members of your family. It may seem too challenging, or they may be scared and unsure. I hope to reassure you that it's going to be okay. Everything is, as I love to say, "figure-out-able."

Be sure to explain to your concerned family members the importance of their role in learning and using ASL with your child. They may not need it right away, but it will be vital for your child's connection, feeling of belonging, and access to everything that the hearing people around them do.

You don't have to sign perfectly to communicate. You don't have to know everything today. Aim to be about five signs ahead of your child, and you'll know enough. It will come, and as you learn together and sign together, signing will become easier and easier, and the joy that it brings into your lives will far outweigh the fear, worry, and effort.

Look for fun ways to add ASL into your everyday life. There are several websites and apps listed in the Resources section (page 157) specifically for adults wanting to learn ASL.

Deaf Community Etiquette

When you find yourself in the Deaf community, or interacting with a Deaf person, it's important to remember these tips:

- When speaking to a Deaf person, be clear. Don't overenunciate or speak louder or slower.

- Make eye contact, and don't mumble, look away, cover your mouth, or chew.

- Sign where possible. Teach your child to always use sign language when in and around the Deaf community.

- Speak directly to the other person, even if an interpreter is there. Don't say things like "Tell her that . . . ." Speak to them, and the interpreter will sign it for you.

- Be respectful of other people's choices to use or not use hearing aids or cochlear implants. It's a much-debated topic in the Deaf community.

- If you are at a Deaf event, be sure to sign as much as you can with everyone. It is rude to have a conversation with another hearing person without signing when you are in full view of others who are Deaf.

- Feel free to introduce yourself and reach out. Deaf people love to chat. You can ask for help and guidance. Be respectful and grateful for their time.

- Deaf people are often blunt and direct. They comfortably discuss topics that most hearing people think of as taboo. Their bluntness rarely comes from ill intentions. It is quite freeing to let go of social norms and expectations in an open conversation.

The most important things to remember are to treat them as regular people and to be inclusive.

Finding an ASL Community

While it's most important for your family to learn signing together, it's equally important for your child to experience sign language outside the home.

You can go to local Deaf events together; find them by reaching out to local support groups you find online, or perhaps on the bulletin board at your local library or community center, and by reaching out to any local colleges with ASL teachers.

Don't be afraid to form an ASL kids' signing group with other Deaf kids or children with ASD, with hearing children, or with a mix of all types and ages. Reach out to your friends with children of a similar age. You can have an ASL teacher come and teach the class, you can teach the class, or you can play ASL DVDs that teach signs. Afterward, you can play games that involve signing or let the kids play together while the parents interact and ask questions using the signs learned. This will help your child make new friends and provide more children for them to talk to.

As a parent, you may be feeling isolated, as well. Make your own support and care a top priority. Reach out to parents you meet at Deaf events—in particular, speak to other hearing parents. They've been where you are now and can offer priceless advice and support for issues that pop up over the years.

In the Resources (page 157) I have listed a few wonderful places for you to start to make connections, make friends, and give your family, yourself, and your child the support and interaction you each need.

Developmental Milestones

The rate that your child learns ASL depends on several factors:

- Age
- Developmental abilities
- Physical dexterity
- The consistency and frequency of exposure to signing

Only the last factor is in your control. If you put in the time and stay as consistent as possible, your rate of learning will increase. Consistency is often hard to achieve, no matter how important it is to you. Don't beat yourself up if you're struggling with this; keep trying, and eventually it will stick.

If your child is Deaf or hard of hearing, their rate of learning will be rather fast as long as there are no medical or developmental issues in play. Their great desire to communicate—and to know that you understand them and they understand you—will have them learning faster than you can keep up. They may struggle to form signs correctly,

and that is perfectly acceptable. Continue to sign accurately, and learn to recognize their signs and applaud every iteration of the sign, no matter how hard it may be to understand.

If your child has ASD, repetition is key, as are patience and understanding. The more you teach signs that connect to things they most care about and are connected to, the faster they'll learn. Teach concrete objects first, then add in actions, and then try more abstract ideas. Work on individual signs before attempting to combine signs to create complete phrases and sentences. For children with autism, it's important to correct their signs immediately and to progress at their pace. With your direction and consistency, it will become an easier form of communication for them and assist them in becoming verbal, or more verbal than they are now. If they do not imitate your signs at first, keep using the signs. It may take them longer to do so, and that's okay.

If your child is hearing, the rate at which they learn is up to you, the parent, as well as their interest level. Stay consistent, and make it fun. Children love to play games.

2

The First 10 Signs

IN THIS CHAPTER, we're going to ease into learning ASL. We'll go over how to teach the signs, which hand to use, troubleshooting, and practice suggestions, and of course, we'll cover the first 10 signs you need to know.

Each sign will be shown with an illustration, as well as accompanying directions, to make it easier to learn. There are memory tips for retention as well as additional tips to help you use the signs successfully and confidently.

Take this chapter as quickly or as slowly as you desire. You may be inclined to dive straight in, or you may prefer the wading-in method. Do what is best for you and your family, but most of all, make a choice and act.

These first 10 signs will be lifesavers for you and your child. You'll finally be able to communicate the things that can frustrate you most when you don't know what your child wants, what they need, or how to help them. Let's ease that burden and then have even more fun in the following chapters.

How to Teach Signs

These first 10 signs can be learned in a day and may take around a week to master. When you teach your child these signs, be sure to keep your hands visible, be willing to repeat, and be gentle when helping them sign. Praise their efforts, but correct mistakes immediately. If they are having a hard time, take a break and come back to it. The point isn't perfection with their signing but to be as accurate as they can be with their current age and skill set.

Show the sign, link it to an object or action, and repeat the sign several times before prompting them to recreate it. You will need to take their hands and guide their signing at first. Depending on their development, they may not need prompting past the first few weeks of signing.

As suggested in chapter 1, having a special family night to introduce sign language, and to learn a few signs together, is a great way to bring in the spirit of adventure and fun. It also gives you an exact start date, so if you've been dragging your feet, you have a specific day to prepare for.

To make this introduction easier, I've put together a seven-day plan, perfect for those wanting to wade in and take it easy. If you're a jump-straight-into-the-pool type of person, you can use the guidelines outlined but shorten the timeline to fit your needs.

DAY 1

Pick out an ASL DVD or book from the Resources (page 157) and watch or read it together.

Once you've either read the sign language storybook or watched the movie, show each other a favorite sign you learned and practice signing it together.

DAY 2

Teach the signs FOOD (page 18) and DRINK (page 17). There's a fun activity in the Sign Practice section (page 30) you can use for these two signs.

DAY 3

Teach the signs MOM (page 19), DAD (page 20), and ME (page 21).

DAY 4

Teach BATHROOM (page 25) and HOME (page 26).

DAY 5

Teach YES (page 27) and NO (page 28).

DAY 6

Teach I LOVE YOU (page 29).

What parent doesn't want their child to say "I love you" and for their child to know how much they love them? This concept is more abstract, but hugs, kisses, cuddles, showing pictures in books of people hugging, and being loving are wonderful ways to reinforce this sign. Sign this sign often, and cherish those first times your little one initiates the sign all by themselves.

DAY 7

While it would be good to have been repeating the signs you've covered throughout the week, make an extra effort today to go over each sign purposefully. You can repeat the Sign Practice activities to reinforce your learning.

Every time you use a word, read it in a story, or see the object or action occur throughout your day, sign it. If the sign doesn't come up often in your home, look for opportunities to incorporate it into your life with books, songs, pictures, and conversation.

Which Hand to Use

When you write, you are generally right-handed or left-handed. It is the same when you sign; your dominant signing hand is either your right hand or your left hand. Those who are ambidextrous when writing or participating in sports cannot be ambidextrous here. You must choose a hand to be your dominant hand. You will sign with both hands simultaneously, but there is always a dominant hand established.

If your child is anything like my three-year-old and four-year-old, they may not yet have settled on one hand. If they clearly favor a hand, that is their dominant hand for ASL. If they don't, you have a few options:

- You can teach them a few signs and, over a week's time, see which hand they sign most with and go with that hand. This isn't always the best option, since many times they'll mirror you, and it may not be the hand they're most comfortable with.

- Teach them the signs based on the hand they most often eat with when using a fork or spoon.

- Choose for them, and switch only if it becomes evident that they prefer the opposite hand. If you do pick, go for the right hand to be the dominant hand.

Tips for Success

You probably have some questions, and I'd like to address them here before you get too worried about them.

Do you speak while you sign?

That answer varies based on your child's needs and the reasons you are learning ASL. If you are teaching a Deaf or hard of hearing child, the answer is no, you do not speak while you sign.

If your child is hearing, depending on the circumstances for teaching them ASL, you can speak while you sign, but I would encourage you to turn your voice "off." Your child's English language skills will not suffer, as there are plenty of opportunities for you to speak with them.

Everyone can benefit from signing without speaking. ASL is its own language, and, as you will learn, does not follow the rules of English syntax. When you're speaking and signing, it's similar to speaking Mandarin and French at

the same time. If you can imagine that, you can quickly realize it's not going to work.

The exception is for children with ASD: You must speak and sign simultaneously. You may also need to modify some of the signs based on your child's abilities.

When should I be signing?

Sign as often as you can. You may get tired and need a break, and it is okay to take breaks. The more you sign, over time, the fewer breaks you will need and the easier it will be for you to learn ASL and remember it. On top of that, it will become natural for you to sign, helping you make a smooth transition from not signing at all to signing consistently.

If you're learning signs for specific situations and not for fluency, then always sign in those situations.

Should I repeat my signs?

As you are teaching signs to your child, you may find it best to repeat your signs several times in the same scenario. Later on, this need won't be as great. When we are around a hearing child who is learning to speak, we don't repeat words unless we're specifically teaching those words. We repeat it a few times, ask them to say it, and then move on. Treat ASL the same. Repeat it for the first introduction, use it throughout the day, and then after that, use it in regular conversation, naturally, repeating only when you need to clarify or reteach.

For children with ASD, the repetition phase may last longer, or it may continue to be a part of your natural conversation for a long while. It truly depends on your child.

My child has autism. Is learning sign language with them different in any way?

Yes. For children with ASD, you speak and sign at the same time, the order in which you present signs is strategic, and you go at a slower pace. You also may find that you need to modify more complex signs. Throughout this book, I will point out these signs and discuss possible modifications you can use.

Drink

With your dominant hand, make the c handshape and rest the thumb on your chin. Tilt your hand back as if drinking from a cup, leaving the thumb in place.

✳ Memory Tip
It's just like drinking out of a cup.

🧩 Similar Sign
This sign can be confused with **ORANGE** (page 58), which uses a similar handshape and is in front of the mouth.

✅ Signing Tip
You can alter the way you sign **DRINK** by exaggerating the movement and holding the "cup" up while tilting your head back, as if you were waiting for that last drop to slide down your cup into your mouth.

Food

With your dominant hand in a flat o handshape (with all your fingers resting on your thumb), bring it up to your lips and tap twice.

✳ Memory Tip

It's as if you were bringing a sandwich to your mouth.

🐦 Sign Variation

If you sign this by bringing it up to your lips but without tapping twice, it becomes the sign **EAT**.

🔗 Grammar Tip

You can say various things by signing **FOOD** and changing your expression. **NO FOOD** is signed by shaking your head while signing **FOOD**. You can use this to say, "No, you can't have food." Say the opposite by nodding your head and using the sign. To ask if your child wants food, sign it while raising your eyebrows.

Mom

With your dominant hand in the 5 hand-shape, place the thumb just under the corner of the mouth (not directly underneath the nose).

✳ Memory Tip

Female signs are signed around the chin area.

🧩 Similar Sign

This sign can be confused with **GRANDMA** (page 35), **DAD** (page 20), and **GRANDPA** (page 36). The difference between **MOM** and **GRANDMA** is the movement. **DAD** and **GRANDPA** are signed in a different location.

✅ Signing Tip

It's important that you do not sign this directly under the mouth in line with the nose. When signing, we place signs just out of our sight line so we can maintain eye contact and not have signs blocking our own vision.

Dad

With your dominant hand in the 5 hand-shape, place the thumb just above the tail of the eyebrow (not directly above the nose or at the temple).

✳ Memory Tip

Male signs are signed around the forehead area.

❖ Similar Sign

This sign can be confused with **MOM** (page 19), **GRANDMA** (page 35), and **GRANDPA** (page 36). The difference from both **MOM** and **GRANDMA** is the location, and in the sign for **GRANDPA**, the movement is different.

✅ Signing Tip

Make sure to place your hand at the eyebrow so your arm is not blocking your vision. Keep your palm facing the side rather than facing out. If you turn your palm to face out, or away from your body, you are signing **DEER**.

Me

Bring the index finger of your dominant hand to the center of your chest, as if pointing at yourself.

Memory Tip

You are, in fact, pointing at yourself.

Other Meaning

This is also the sign for **I**. The signs **ME**, **MINE**, and **MYSELF** are all located at the chest in the same spot.

Signing Tip

You may have seen this signed with the **I** handshape, with the fist to the chest and the pinkie extended. This is incorrect, as it's Signed Exact English and not ASL.

Troubleshooting

In the beginning, you and your child may find signing difficult. Don't be disheartened or let it stop your progress. Any and all effort you put in will have its reward. Here are some tips for common issues you may come up against.

YOUR CHILD IS DOING THE SIGN WRONG

When you see your child signing, any attempts should be praised and recognized. Continue to sign the sign the proper way, and offer corrections when the moment is right. Just as hearing kids mispronounce and mix up words, so do signing children. Embrace the cuteness, and write down the funny things they do to help you remember it years from now. Signing inaccurately is a normal part of learning sign language and of growing and developing as a child. They'll eventually get it right with enough exposure to correct signing. For children with ASD, you will need to help them sign as accurately as they are capable. Correct often and gently, and take breaks when they need them.

YOUR CHILD IS MIXING UP SIGNS

If your child is mixing up signs, signing one sign when they mean another, know that it's normal and can be fixed. The first thing to do is to understand their meaning using pointing, pictures, and context clues. After you understand what they're communicating, reteach and reinforce the sign. Use some of the practice prompts found throughout the book to practice the sign they forgot. I don't recommend practicing both signs at the same time. Practice the forgotten sign until it's mastered, and then practice the other sign on a completely different day.

Scrolling is common with children who have autism. An example of scrolling is if you hold up a cup and ask, "What is this?" and they scroll through all the possibilities: FOOD, DRINK, CUPCAKE, CUP, and so on. You may think, *"Well, they did finally sign* CUP," and praise them, but doing this confuses them and cements this scrolling response. Put their hands down to a neutral position, and physically prompt the sign. You want to spend the majority of your time preventing errors.

YOUR CHILD HAS STOPPED SIGNING

This may be alarming and bring up a lot of doubt and worry. Take a deep breath, remind yourself that you can figure this out, and then proceed. Your child may stop signing for a few reasons, including not getting the desired reaction from parents, frustration with not knowing how to sign something, mental exhaustion, or physical strain.

First, check to see if they're tired. Do they need a break? You'll want to verify there are no physical limitations or injuries. If there are, consult your doctor for guidance. If it is exhaustion, give yourselves a fun break. Have quiet time, look at books together, or play outside. Do something that doesn't require much language, and just be together. Allow your child to be refreshed and ready to sign again.

They may be eager to sign something but meet with frustration when they don't know how. You can test this out by finding ways to introduce signs covering new topics and ideas that may interest them. If they begin to sign again, then you'll know that it's important to them to have new signs added to their toolbox regularly.

The most common explanation is that their attempts at signing aren't recognized by their parents. They may be signing inaccurately, by either not doing a sign correctly or mixing up signs, and the parent doesn't recognize it. Do not beat yourself up; this happens to parents in every culture. Spend time taking extra care to observe their behavior and movements. If they are repeating movements, they're most likely signing.

TIPS FOR DEAF AND HARD OF HEARING CHILDREN

Your little one will be so excited to have access to language that you may find them asking how to sign anything and everything they can think of. Let your child's interests and questions guide you. Don't feel constrained by chapters and order. You can use these chapters to guide your repetition and reinforcement, as your child may forget a sign or get mixed up. Don't rein in their desire to learn; instead, run with it.

TIPS FOR CHILDREN WITH ASD

Start with five signs. I recommend two food items, one drink, and two more signs that have meaning to them.

Avoid teaching signs like MORE, PLEASE, and THANK YOU. You want to teach concrete and specific signs at the beginning. Manners can be taught later.

Don't teach signs that look similar to one another at the same time. When you do teach a sign that is similar to a previously taught sign, be aware of it and look for mix-ups and confusion.

Learn simple signs first rather than more complex signs. Depending on your child, you may need to permanently modify complex signs.

Everyone in the family needs to both speak and sign words the same way. This will make teaching and reinforcing signs easier.

Prompt your child to sign before giving them the item requested. Each time they sign a request—for instance, JUICE (page 75)—give it to them immediately, once signed correctly.

Bathroom

With your dominant hand, hold your hand up in the т handshape (page 149), and shake it from side to side. The shake is a bending motion of your wrist.

✳ **Memory Tip**
T stands for toilet.

❞ **Other Meaning**
You can use this sign for **BATHROOM**, **TOILET**, and **RESTROOM**.

🧩 **Similar Sign**
This sign can be confused with the sign **WHERE**. The only difference between the two is in the handshape; **WHERE** is signed with the **1** handshape.

Home

With your dominant hand, place all your fingers on your thumb in a flat o hand-shape. Touch your fingertips to the side of your mouth, near the corner, and then touch the top of your cheekbone, near your ear.

✳ Memory Tip

This is in reference to where you eat and sleep. It's a shortened version of **EAT** (page 18) and **BED** (page 84), using the same handshape as for the sign **EAT**.

🧩 Similar Sign

This sign can be confused with the sign for **DEAF** (page 136), which is signed in the same location and manner but with the index finger.

🔗 Grammar Tip

To say "We're going home," you would sign **HOME** and then **GO** (page 139). To ask if your child wants to go home, you still sign **HOME GO**, but raise your eyebrows while you sign **GO**.

Yes

With your dominant hand, make the s handshape, hold it up, and nod its "head" twice.

✳ Memory Tip

The hand is mimicking a head nodding up and down.

✅ Signing Tip

To show an emphatic **YES**, nod it just once with an exaggerated movement.

💕 ASD Tip

For children with ASD, be careful when introducing the concept of **YES**. Wait until they can request about a dozen items, both seen and unseen.

No

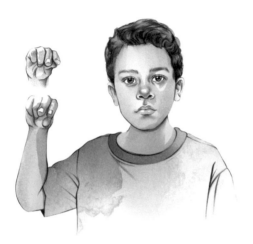

This is a combination of the letters **N** and **O** opening and closing to sign **NO** quickly.

✓ **Signing Tip**

When signing **NO**, shake your head. You can increase the intensity of the meaning either by repeating the tapping more than twice or by snapping the fingers together (and starting from a wider starting position) in anger.

💝 **ASD Tip**

For children with ASD, you can teach **NO** early. This is ideal for replacing behaviors such as crying and pushing items away.

Using your dominant hand, hold the index finger and middle finger together, sticking out, with the thumb also sticking out. Tap the fingertips to the thumb twice, as if it were a duck's bill opening and closing.

I love you

Hold the dominant hand up, with the pinkie, index finger, and thumb extended.

✳ Memory Tip

This is a combination of the handshapes **I**, **L**, and **Y**, which stand for "I love you."

🛫 Sign Variation

This is the casual meaning of "I love you." This is a very common sign used within the Deaf community as more of a friendly greeting, when waving goodbye to friends, and when posing for pictures (similar to people using the peace sign in pictures). To show a deeper love, sign the official sign for **LOVE**, which is both hands in the **S** handshape, crossed over the chest, with hands on your shoulders. Combine this with the signs **I** (page 148) and **YOU** (page 40) and you have the entire phrase.

✓ Signing Tip

You can wave with this sign, one-handed or with both hands, to say goodbye. If you circle the index finger while keeping the other fingers still, it means "I always love you."

Sign Practice

Here are some suggested activities for practicing these first signs with your child.

INTRODUCING FOOD AND DRINK

Prepare a special treat and favorite drink for the family to enjoy. When you pull out the treat, sign **FOOD** (page 18). Point to the treat, and sign **FOOD** again. Hand your child the treat, and sign **FOOD**.

Now, you can either prompt them to sign it or take their hand and help them sign it. Be gentle as you take their hand.

Each of you takes turns signing **FOOD** as you lift, eat, or point to your treat.

Repeat this same process with your drink.

INTRODUCING PEOPLE

Pull out printed pictures, or digital pictures on your phone, and make a fun game of finding all the pictures with mom, dad, and your child. Each time you happen upon a picture of mom, sign **MOM** (page 19). When you see dad, sign **DAD** (page 20). When you see your child, you can sign **ME** (page 21).

You can, of course, sign **ME** when it is conceptually accurate to sign **ME**.

INTRODUCING PLACES

Throughout the day, take them into the bathroom, even if they're not potty trained, and sign **BATHROOM** (page 25) each time, prompting them to do the same.

To practice **HOME** (page 26), you can go on a walk around the block, and each time you reach your home, sign **HOME**. You can also show a picture of your house and sign **HOME** throughout the day, because I'm sure you'll not want to walk around the block all day!

INTRODUCING YES AND NO

Start introducing these signs as you would naturally say them in various situations. To make it more fun, you can play a matching game or a puzzle.

Hold up a pair of cards that don't match, and sign **NO** (page 28). Be expressive and exaggerate your **NO** with your face, shaking your head, and be fun about it. This isn't lecture time.

Now, take one of those cards and match it correctly with another card. Sign **YES** (page 27), again being very expressive. You can find things around the house to illustrate these points. Do they know already not to touch the stove? You can head over there and sign **NO**, and then find something in the kitchen they are allowed to touch and sign **YES**.

Do this whenever you can, signing **YES** and **NO** each time and helping them do the same, until you can see the concept has clicked. They may start running around the house finding things to say yes and no to. Jumping on the couch? **NO!** Jumping on the trampoline? **YES!**

If your child has autism, do this activity with **NO**, and skip teaching **YES** until they're ready for this harder concept.

Continuing Your ASL Journey

You made it through the first 10 signs. I'm thrilled for you and your family to officially be signers. I encourage you to use this book however you desire. Here are a few ideas:

- Go through each chapter, one at a time, following the same general pattern of two new signs a day.
- Use the Index (page 159) to find the specific signs you are interested in learning first, until you've learned them all.
- Pick a chapter that has signs that most interest you or your child, focus on those for the week or until you master them, and then pick another chapter to learn.

It's important to focus on mastery of the signs rather than how fast you're learning them. The more comfortable and confident you both are with the signs you learn, the easier it will be to add new signs to your vocabulary.

You can find the ASL alphabet and numbers in chapter 8 (page 147). The alphabet is used for fingerspelling, and even young children can begin to fingerspell and recognize fingerspelled words. Counting in ASL is different from the typical counting with all 10 fingers you see in the hearing world. As recommended earlier, you (but not your child) should learn the alphabet and numbers before learning the signs, as they are critical components of many signs.

3

Family and Feelings

IN ORDER TO help you and your child build relationships within your family and with each other, you're going to learn family and feeling signs. Your child will feel more in control when they can successfully name their feelings and share them with their family members.

In chapter 2, you learned three family signs: **MOM** (page 19), **DAD** (page 20), and **ME** (page 21). In this chapter, you will learn nine more family signs. You will also learn nine feeling signs.

There are many more feeling signs you can learn, but these are the most important for your child to learn first. They are the emotions and feelings your child will most readily identify with and experience throughout their day. Labeling the emotions they feel is the first step to teaching them how to handle their feelings and express appropriate behavior around them.

Throughout this section there are several suggestions for how to introduce these signs to your child in order to make the connection between the sign and the meaning.

Family

Bring both hands in the ꜰ handshape in front of your body. Make a circle with your hands to bring your pinkies to touch so that your palms are facing your body.

✳ Memory Tip

It's as though you're drawing a circle of people with *F* for *family*.

Sign Variation

The movement of this sign is used to indicate various types of groups. You change the type by changing the handshape used: **F** for **FAMILY**, **G** for **GROUP**, **T** for **TEAM**, **C** for **CLASS** or **CLUB**, and so on.

💡 Teaching Tip

Show your child several pictures of your family and other families to connect the sign to its meaning. This may be a harder concept for children to understand; repetition will be important, as will using it in natural conversations.

Grandma

✳ Memory Tip

The two-part movement represents **MOM** (page 19) times 2.

✂ Similar Sign

This sign can be confused with **GRANDPA** (page 36) and with **MOM**. **MOM** is a single tap, while **GRANDMA** adds an arcing movement. **GRANDPA** is signed at the forehead.

💡 Teaching Tip

Children will need help with this movement. Some may mix this sign up with **MOM**, **DAD** (page 20), or **GRANDPA**. Younger signers may struggle to get their thumb on their chin. Help them place their thumb on their chin and make the correct handshape.

With your dominant hand in the 5 hand-shape, bring your thumb up to your chin, making sure to place your thumb to the side of your chin and not in line with your nose. Then bring your hand out in an arc away from your face.

Grandpa

 Memory Tip

The two-part movement represents **DAD** (page 20) times 2.

Similar Sign

This sign can be confused with **GRANDMA** (page 35) and with **DAD**. **DAD** is a single tap, whereas **GRANDPA** adds an arcing movement. **GRANDMA** is signed at the chin.

Teaching Tip

Children will need help with this movement. Some may mix this sign up with **MOM** (page 19), **DAD**, or **GRANDMA**. Younger signers may struggle to get their thumb on their forehead and arc it out. Help them place their thumb on their forehead, making sure it's to the side.

With your dominant hand in the 5 hand-shape, bring your thumb up to your forehead, just above the tail of your eyebrow. Make sure to place your thumb to the side of your forehead and not in line with your nose. Bring your hand out in an arc away from your face.

Sister

Begin with both hands in the A handshape, with the nondominant hand in front of your body and the dominant hand starting at the side of your chin. Bring your dominant hand down on top of your nondominant hand while opening up both hands into the 1 handshape. This is a fluid movement.

✳ Memory Tip

This sign is the abbreviation of **GIRL** and **SAME**, as in girl in the same family.

✓ Signing Tip

This sign can feel tricky at first. Make sure your dominant hand begins at the side of your chin, with the thumb touching the chin. As your hand comes down, form the 1 handshape with both hands simultaneously. The most common errors are switching hands around and mixing it up with the sign **BROTHER** (page 38).

💕 ASD Tip

Children with autism may struggle with this multistep sign. Wait to introduce this sign until they're ready to master the more complex signs. You can test this out and see how well they do, but if it's giving them trouble, skip it until they're ready.

Brother

Begin with both hands in the A handshape, with the nondominant hand in front of your body and the dominant hand starting at the side of your forehead. Bring your dominant hand down on top of your nondominant hand while opening up both hands into the 1 handshape. This is a fluid movement.

✳ Memory Tip

This sign is the abbreviation of **BOY** and **SAME**, as in boys in the same family.

✚ Similar Sign

BROTHER is often mixed up with the sign **SISTER** (page 37) because they are so similar to one another. Take your time to master the movement of this sign, and help your child form the handshapes and move through it. You may also see people sign this starting with the **L** handshape instead of the **A** handshape. You can use this variation if it's easier for your child.

🔗 Grammar Tip

If you want to sign plural **BROTHERS**, you can sign **BROTHER** twice with a slight shift in your body to the right (if you're right-handed; if you're left-handed, shift to the left). You can also sign **BROTHER** and point in a sweeping arch to the side, which is the sign for the plural form of **YOU** (page 40). The same can be used for **SISTER**.

Baby

Place your dominant hand on top of the forearm of your nondominant hand and rock back and forth once.

✳ Memory Tip

This sign looks as though you're cradling a baby in your arms.

✓ Signing Tip

It's a good idea to teach the sign **SOFT** (page 49) when you teach this sign. That way you can help your child associate being gentle and soft with a baby.

💡 Teaching Tip

Children love to sign **BABY**. It's a fun sign, and they love to point out babies. Use picture books of babies to introduce the sign. You can even show your child pictures of themselves as a baby. They'll be so excited to sign **BABY** when they see a real baby.

You

With your dominant hand in the 1 hand-shape, point at the person you are signing to.

✳ Memory Tip

This sign is pretty easy to remember—you're simply pointing at the other person.

🙶 Other Meaning

This sign is also used for **HE**, **SHE**, and **IT**. The only difference is the direction you point.

🔗 Grammar Tip

YOU is directional, meaning you point to the person you're signing to, wherever they are. If they're to your left, point to your left. The general use of this sign—for a nonspecific *you*—is signed as if the person you're talking about is standing directly in front of you.

They

✳ Memory Tip

You're pointing to several people as though they were standing side by side in a small cluster.

✓ Signing Tip

If you are left-handed, start with your arm pointing across to the right and sweep it to your left side.

⬙ Grammar Tip

You can use this to point to an actual group of people, and if you do, point to where they are located. You can also use this sign to talk about a group of people who are not present.

With the index finger of your dominant hand extended across the body, pointing to the side, sweep your hand toward the opposite side, in an arc, keeping the palm facing the side. This is a small sweeping movement.

Us

Using the index finger of your dominant hand, touch one shoulder and then, making a small arc, touch the other shoulder.

✱ Memory Tip

It's as if you were signing **THEY** (page 41) but toward your body, to include yourself in the group.

 Other Meaning

This is also the sign for **WE**.

💡 Teaching Tip

This may be a harder-concept sign for some children to understand at first. Use this sign naturally, and your child will pick up on the meaning as they would any other word. If you have the chance to point out two groups of people, us and them (they), this can help introduce the concept.

Happy

Bring the flat palm of your dominant hand up to tap the area directly above your chest (below your collarbone, but not on your chest). You will tap it twice, using a circular motion to bring your hand up, out, and back to the same spot to tap the second time. You may also see this sign two-handed, with the nondominant hand at the belly.

✳ Memory Tip

It shows the feeling of joy bursting out of your chest.

❞ Other Meaning

This is also the sign for **JOY**.

✚ Similar Sign

This sign is often mixed up with **PLEASE** (page 123) and **EXCITED**. **PLEASE** uses a clockwise motion, and **EXCITED** uses a different handshape but similar movement.

Sad

With both hands in the 5 handshape with palms facing you and just in front of your face, bring them down from the tops of your cheeks to your chin.

✳ Memory Tip

You're showing tears flowing down your face.

✚ Similar Sign

This sign can be mixed up with CRY and with TIGER. CRY is done with your hands in the 1 handshape, running down your face like individual tears, and TIGER is the same hand-shape but drawing stripes across your cheeks rather than down your cheeks.

✔ Signing Tip

It's important to have your facial expression match the meaning of this sign. Use a sad face to make the message clear. This is part of the sign.

Hug

Place each of your hands, which are in the A handshape, just above the crook of the opposite elbow. Squeeze your hands into your body and bring up your shoulders at the same time, as if you're hugging yourself tight.

✳ Memory Tip
You're hugging yourself.

✦ Similar Signs
This sign can be confused with **LOVE** (page 29). **HUG** is lower on the arms, while **LOVE** is signed at the shoulders.

💡 Teaching Tip
This is a fun sign to teach. Get ready for a lot of hugs with your child. Repeat the sign several times, and initiate a hug. Sign it again, and hug again. Prompt your child to sign **HUG**, and then give them a hug. Play the hugging game: You and your child can take turns hugging things you love around your house. One person signs **HUG** and points to the object; the other hugs it. You can hug things like your favorite food, toy, picture, pillow, tree, animal, and so on.

Scared

✳ Memory Tip

This abrupt opening of the hands mimics the body freezing when scared.

❞ Other Meaning

This is the sign for all forms of the word *scared*: **TERRIFIED**, **FREAKED OUT**, and other related synonyms. The more you exaggerate your facial expression, the more you show how scared you are.

✅ Signing Tip

Be sure to clench your teeth and widen your eyes as though you're scared.

Start with both hands in the s handshape, one in front of the chest and the other in front of the belly, palms facing you. Bring your hands toward each other while abruptly opening them into the 5 handshape.

Facial Expressions

As you have noticed throughout this chapter, many signs require accompanying facial expressions. This is very common in ASL.

Facial expressions are a major part of ASL grammar. Just as your voice uses inflection and pace to give meaning to the words you're speaking, in sign language we use our facial expressions and body language to bring meaning to our signs.

They are vital, and in several instances, signing the exact same sign but with a change in facial expression changes the entire meaning. You will see an example of this with the sign SOFT (page 49). Change the facial expression, and it means WET.

You can use a negative facial expression or a shake of the head to change a sign from a positive meaning to its negation. This method can be used in teaching your child the negative version of a sign before introducing NO (page 28). For instance, you can sign FOOD (page 18) and shake your head to mean NO FOOD.

If your child has ASD and does not produce facial expressions easily or at all, do not be discouraged. Continue to sign to them with the appropriate facial expressions. The negating of signs with facial expressions may be confusing to them, or they may miss the entire meaning. Introduce negative facial expressions when they're ready. When expressing all other emotions, continue to use matching facial expressions.

Angry

With your dominant hand in the 5 hand-shape in front of your nose and mouth, bend your fingers quickly, twice, as if grabbing a ball that's too big for your hand and squeezing it a bit.

✳ Memory Tip

This is like the scrunching and changing of a person's face when they are angry.

🙿 Other Meaning

This sign is used for many variations of angry moods, including **GROUCHY**, **GRUMPY**, and **CRANKY**.

✛ Similar Sign

This sign is similar to **HOT** and **WARM** (page 90), which use the same handshape and are in the same location. The difference between the three signs is in the movements.

✅ Signing Tip

Furrow your eyebrows and look angry when signing this.

Soft

Memory Tip

It's as if you were squeezing cotton candy in your hands.

Other Meaning

This sign is used for **SOFT**, **GENTLE**, and **TENDER**. Make your facial expression neutral or happy.

Similar Sign

If you sign this with your lips in an "eww" shape, it becomes the sign for **WET** or **DAMP**.

Hold both hands in front of you with the palms facing up and all the fingers bent so they are pointing up. Bring both hands downward and the fingertips together to form flat o handshapes. This movement is short and is done twice.

Sorry

With your dominant hand in the s hand-shape, place it on your chest and move it in a circle twice.

✳ Memory Tip

S stands for *sorry*, near your heart, as though apologizing from the heart.

❢❢ Other Meaning

This sign can be used for **I'M SORRY**, **SAY YOU'RE SORRY**, and **APOLOGIZE**.

✅ Signing Tip

This sign is typically two small circles. However, if you're using it to apologize to someone, you can sign in a slightly bigger and slower movement to show extra sincerity.

Help

✳ Memory Tip

The bottom hand is helping the top hand.

✓ Signing Tip

Raise your eyebrows and lean your head forward slightly to make this a question. While doing this, move the sign from your body toward the other person's body to ask, "Can I help you?"

⌖ Grammar Tip

HELP is a directional sign. The handshapes remain the same, but the movement changes to mean different things. To sign **YOU HELP ME**, start the sign from farther away from your body and bring it to your stomach in a straight line. To sign **I HELP YOU**, start from your stomach and push your hands out, in a straight line, toward the person you're signing to. The starting position is the person doing the helping, and the ending position is the person being helped.

Place your nondominant hand in front of you, just above your belly button, in a flat handshape with the palm facing up. Place your dominant hand on top of the palm, in a 10 handshape with the thumb pointing up. Bring both hands up in a short movement.

Hurt

Start with both hands in the 1 handshape with the palms facing your body, index fingers pointing toward each other, just in front of the body part that hurts. Bring the index fingers toward each other while simultaneously twisting in opposite directions.

✳ Memory Tip

The fingers twisting conveys irritation.

❖ Similar Sign

This sign can mean **HURT** or **PAIN** in a general sense. If you want to show you have pain in a specific part of your body, do the sign in front of that part. If you sign it in front of the head, it means **HEADACHE**. Sign it on the stomach to mean **STOMACHACHE**. If it's lower on your body, for instance, your foot, you would point to the foot and then sign **HURT**.

✓ Signing Tip

Be sure to use a matching facial expression to show pain. Squinting the eyebrows and pursing the lips is a common expression.

Sign Practice

SIGN A STORY

Look for a book about families to read to your child. When you come to family members that you know the signs for, sign them and then prompt your child to do the same. Three good books to read together are *Goldilocks and the Three Bears*, *Families* by Ann Morris, and *Families Are Different* by Nina Pellegrini.

SIGN AND SING

To the tune of "Hickory Dickory Dock," sing this fun emotions song together and sign the emotions you have learned as you sing those words.

How are you feeling today?
Oh, how are you feeling today?
I'm happy and glad, happy and glad,
That's how I'm feeling today.

Repeat with different emotions, such as grumpy and cross, or crying and sad.

EMOTIONS CRAFT

With your child, make a variety of faces to match the emotion signs you've learned so far using felt, googly eyes, yarn, and popsicle sticks. Cut the felt into circles, and glue on the eyes. Help them make the eyebrows and mouths with the yarn to match the emotion being portrayed. Once their faces are finished, add yarn hair and glue the faces to the popsicle sticks. Play with your finished stick people, and sign the emotion each face shows. You can use them with the emotions song, as well. When your child is having trouble expressing their feelings, you can bring out the popsicle sticks and help them identify their emotion and sign it, as well. This is a wonderful opportunity to teach feelings and to practice signing.

4

Mealtime

IN CHAPTER 2, you learned the general signs for **FOOD** (page 18) and **DRINK** (page 17). In this chapter, you'll learn many specific food signs and three types of drinks.

This chapter is one of the longest, with 23 signs. Take your time going through each sign, focusing on retaining and using the signs you've learned before moving to the next one. If there are foods your family doesn't eat or like, it's okay to skip learning those signs. You can come back and learn them at a later time, after you've learned the most important signs for your family.

You can combine these signs with those you learned in chapters 2 and 3 to create phrases and provide additional meaning. These are good signs to use for practicing responding with **YES** (page 27) and **NO** (page 28). Most children are eager to tell their parents which foods they will and won't eat. Take advantage of this to reemphasize their grasp on those two signs.

Apple

With your dominant hand in a fist, stick out the knuckle of your index finger. Place the knuckle near the corner of your mouth, where a dimple would be, and twist twice.

✳ Memory Tip

Think of the apple of your cheeks.

✙ Similar Sign

This sign can be mixed up with **ONION**, which uses the same handshape and movement but is placed by the corner of the eye, because onions make you cry.

💡 Teaching Tip

Introduce this sign during snack time. Show a whole apple and sign **APPLE**, then cut it into slices. Show a slice, and sign it again. Help your child sign **APPLE**, and then hand them a slice. Prompt them to sign **APPLE** before you hand them the next slice.

Banana

Hold your nondominant hand in the ı handshape, while your dominant hand in a flat o handshape moves from the tip of the opposite finger to the base, twice.

 **Memory Tip**

You are peeling a banana.

Grammar Tip

If you want to offer your child a banana, raise your eyebrows and lean your head slightly forward. This makes the sign **BANANA** mean "Do you want a banana?" Or you can nod your head while signing **BANANA** to mean "Yes, you can have a banana" or shake your head while signing to mean "No, you can't have a banana."

Teaching Tip

Introduce this sign with a snack of bananas, or make banana pudding together. You can make this a special dessert for the family. Have your child teach everyone the sign while serving each person a cup of pudding.

Orange

✱ Memory Tip
You are holding an orange to your mouth to squeeze out the juice.

🗨 Other Meaning
This sign is used for both the fruit and the color.

🧩 Similar Sign
This sign can be mixed up with **APPLE** (page 56) and **MILK** (page 76). **ORANGE** and **MILK** use the same shape and movement but are in different locations. **APPLE** is also signed near the mouth.

Start with your dominant hand in front of your mouth in an open s handshape, then close it to the s handshape. Do this movement twice.

Grape

Start with your nondominant hand in the s handshape and your dominant hand in the 5 handshape but with all the fingers bent, forming a claw. Tap the fingertips of your dominant hand near the wrist on the back of your nondominant hand. Then lift your fingertips and tap the middle of your hand, and lift them again and tap near the knuckles. (You're tapping the back of your hand three times.)

✷ **Memory Tip**

You're showing clusters of grapes on the back of your hand.

✅ **Signing Tip**

This sign can be tricky for your child to get exactly right. Help them make the movements with their hand. If they tap in the same location, or only once, guide them through the motion. You can also hold their "claw" hand and move it down the back of your **s** hand to help them do the sign on a bigger hand.

💡 **Teaching Tip**

Have a cluster of grapes with you when you introduce this sign. Sign it a few times before helping your child form the sign. You can take your "claw" hand and do the sign down the cluster of grapes to connect the shape of the grapes to the handshape and movement.

Chicken

Hold the index finger and thumb of your dominant hand at the corner of your mouth. Open and close your fingers two times.

* Memory Tip

This sign mimics a chicken's beak.

🙾 Other Meaning

This is the sign for both the animal and the form of chicken that you eat. Since it means both, you may want to choose one or the other to introduce first to avoid confusion. It is also used to sign **BIRD**.

🔁 Sign Variation

You may want to sign **CHICKEN NUGGETS**. There is no official sign for *nuggets*, but you can sign **CHICKEN** and then form two circles with your index fingers and thumbs and show them next to one another. Tuck the rest of your fingers into a fist shape; you don't want your hands in the **F** handshape, with your fingers sticking out.

Pizza

Your hand is a slice of pizza and you're bringing it to your mouth to eat.

Sign Variation
There are multiple ways to sign PIZZA, but this is the more common version you will see within the Deaf community.

Teaching Tip
Make homemade pizza together, or pick up your favorite pie to go. Every time someone takes a slice of pizza, everyone signs PIZZA!

This sign can feel awkward the first few times you sign it. With your dominant hand in a flat handshape, with the palm facing up and the thumb extended, bring it toward your mouth. You'll need to raise your elbow out to the side to do this sign without injury to your wrist.

Hot dog

Hold both of your hands in an open s handshape next to each other in front of your body. Close them into an s handshape, then open and close them again while moving them out in opposite directions, then do this again, moving them farther away from each other.

✳ Memory Tip
You are showing sausages linked together.

🎯 Other Meaning
This sign is used for **HOT DOG**, **SAUSAGE**, and any meat in tube form. To differentiate those unique meats, you would sign **HOT DOG** and then fingerspell the specific name of the meat you are talking about.

💔 ASD Tip
The dual movement of the hands opening and closing and moving outward in opposite directions may be tricky for children with ASD or younger children. You may need to demonstrate the sign several times before you help them form it themselves. Place your hands over their fists and squeeze and release when they're supposed to close and open their hands. As you do this, move their hands out with each squeeze.

Sandwich

Form your nondominant hand into a sideways pocket with your four fingers together. It should look like you're making a hand puppet. Slip your dominant hand into the space between your opposite fingers and thumb, and bring both hands to your lips. You don't need to open your mouth.

✳ Memory Tip

Your nondominant hand is the bread and your dominant hand is the filling of the sandwich, and you're about to take a bite.

▪ Similar Sign

This sign is similar to **TACO**, but **TACO** is held out in front of the body with the palm of the nondominant hand facing up.

⌘ Grammar Tip

Ask your child if they want a sandwich by raising your eyebrows and leaning your head forward a bit as you sign **SANDWICH**. You can sign additional signs to specify the type of sandwich.

Cracker

✳ Memory Tip

This is a funny sign, but you can remember it by thinking of the cracking sound a cracker would make if you knocked on it with your fist.

🗩 Other Meaning

Use this sign with a bunch of different crackers—Goldfish, graham crackers, cheese crackers, and any other type of cracker your child likes—to show they all use the same sign.

🧩 Similar Sign

This sign can be mixed up with **COUNTRY**, which is signed in the same location but with a different movement and handshape for the dominant hand.

Hold your nondominant hand in the s handshape across your body, near the opposite shoulder. With your dominant hand, also in the s handshape, knock on the opposite elbow, twice.

Carrot

Using your dominant hand, do the same movement you do when signing HOT DOG (page 62), except start at the corner of your mouth. Your teeth will bite down a bit with each squeezing of the hand.

✳ Memory Tip

You are eating a carrot as if you were Bugs Bunny.

🧩 Similar Sign

CARROT can be confused with ORANGE (page 58) since it uses a similar opening and closing of the hand and is near the mouth.

🔀 Sign Variation

You may see people sign CARROT in a variety of ways. Some will do the same movement but toward the mouth, some will do one big bite while bending their hand as if breaking the carrot off, and some will look as though one index finger is peeling the other index finger as if with a vegetable peeler. They're all correct, with the one in this book being the most updated version of the sign. If the majority of people in your community use a different version of the sign, use the one they prefer.

Peas

With your dominant hand in the x hand-shape, tap along the index finger of the nondominant hand in three spots.

✱ Memory Tip

You are tapping on the peas inside a pea pod.

❚❚ Other Meaning

You may see some people use this sign for BEAN, but it is not the official sign; instead, you would fingerspell BEAN.

💡 Teaching Tip

You can use this sign with individual peas and with snap peas. When introducing the sign, start with the form of the vegetable your child is most familiar with.

Bread

Hold your nondominant hand in front of your body so your palm faces your chest. With your dominant hand bent at a 90-degree angle, draw three lines down the back of your nondominant hand with the fingertips. Start from the wrist and move toward the knuckles.

✳ Memory Tip

The nondominant hand represents the loaf of bread, and you're cutting it into slices.

💡 Teaching Tip

Bake a loaf of bread together (or buy one). Demonstrate cutting the bread, and then sign BREAD. Show your child how slicing the bread is similar to how you sign BREAD. This connection may be lost on younger children, but older kids will be able to understand easily.

💟 ASD Tip

Help your child draw the slices on their hand, as this may be tricky. You may have them do just one slice rather than the typical three.

Egg

 Memory Tip

It's like an eggshell being cracked open and separated.

Teaching Tip

Cook eggs with your child. If you have a few eggs to spare, have them crack some open, making sure they sign **EGG** correctly before and then again afterward. This will be a messy lesson they won't forget.

Using the numbers in chapter 8 (page 147), you can count eggs in the carton together. Sign the number and then **EGG** for each egg you count. Have fun with it, and don't worry about the numbers being accurate, but instead focus on the time together and the sign for **EGG** being done correctly.

With both of your hands in the н hand-shape, cross them to form an *X* with the fingertips pointing down. Uncross the fingers so they are pointing straight down a few inches apart.

Cereal

With the dominant hand in the 1 hand-shape, wriggle the index finger horizontally across your chin like a worm.

✳ Memory Tip

Think of the mess cereal can make underneath your lips.

❝ Other Meaning

This sign is also used for **OATMEAL**, and you can also use it for **CREAM OF WHEAT**.

✦ Similar Sign

CEREAL can be confused with **DRY** and **RUSSIA** since both are signed at the chin with a similar handshape and movement. **DRY** moves in the opposite direction with one movement, rather than wriggling. **RUSSIA** is similar to **DRY**, but it flicks out away from the face after drawing across the chin.

Yogurt

Hold your dominant hand in a Y hand-shape in front of your body with the palm facing you, as if about to say "hang loose." Bend the thumb down as if you were pushing a button, twice.

✳ Memory Tip

Y is for *yogurt*.

🧩 Similar Sign

This sign can be mixed up with the sign for **YELLOW**, which is made by shaking the **Y** hand-shape at the side of the body.

💡 Teaching Tip

For a meal or snack, have a couple yogurt tubes and sign **YOGURT**, and have your child sign it, as well. Hand your child a tube, and each time you both drink some of the **YOGURT**, sign the sign together.

Cheese

✳ **Memory Tip**

This sign represents the process of cheese being made.

🧩 **Similar Sign**

This sign can be confused with **PAPER** and **SCHOOL**. All three of these signs use the same handshape and meet together palm to palm. The difference is in the movement: **CHEESE** is twisting, **PAPER** clap-slides backward toward the arm, and **SCHOOL** claps the dominant hand on the heel of the nondominant hand like a teacher getting the class's attention.

✅ **Signing Tip**

Follow this sign with **PIZZA** (page 61), **BURGER**, or **SANDWICH** (page 63) to sign **CHEESE PIZZA**, **CHEESEBURGER**, or **CHEESE SANDWICH**. You can do this with other types of food; for example, after signing **CHEESE**, sign **CAKE** (see Similar Sign on page 73) for **CHEESECAKE**.

Both hands are in the 5 handshape, with the nondominant hand palm up and the dominant hand palm down. Place the heels of the hands together with the fingers of each hand pointed in opposite directions, and twist the dominant hand a few times.

Potato

With your nondominant hand in the s handshape and your dominant hand in a bent v handshape, tap the fingertips of the dominant hand on the back of the nondominant hand, twice.

✳ Memory Tip

It's like sticking a fork into a potato.

❞ Other Meaning

This sign is also used to mean the state of **IDAHO**.

🤸 Sign Variation

Use this sign for the many varieties of potatoes—red, purple, sweet, baby, and baking—but not for French fries. To sign **MASHED POTATOES**, you can make a fist with your dominant hand and "mash" it into the open palm of your nondominant hand, or simply fingerspell *mashed* after signing potato.

Cookie

With your nondominant hand in a flat handshape and your dominant hand in a bent 5 handshape, tap the dominant hand on the palm of the nondominant hand and twist it clockwise, then tap the palm again.

❋ Memory Tip

This motion mimics using a cookie cutter.

◆ Similar Sign

This sign can be mixed up with **CAKE**. When signing **CAKE**, the dominant hand slides up the palm with a similar handshape, to mimic the shape of a slice of cake.

💡 Teaching Tip

You can really have fun teaching this sign. Make sugar cookies together, so you can roll out the cookie dough and use various cookie cutters. Sign **COOKIE** when you cut out a cookie and when you place one on the baking sheet. When you pull the cookies out of the oven to cool and decorate, sign **COOKIE**. Of course, when you feast on your treats, continue to sign **COOKIE**.

Water

With your dominant hand in the w handshape, tap the index finger to the side of the mouth.

✳ Memory Tip

W stands for *water*, and it's near the mouth, where you drink.

🟄 Other Meaning

This sign stands for all forms of water: water you drink, bathwater, a pool, an ocean, or a lake. Many signs use the sign **WATER** in combination with other signs to talk about various bodies of water and even ice.

💡 Teaching Tip

Take your child outside for water play. Use buckets, a baby pool, cups, colanders, and any other toys your child likes to play with. Fill your containers with water, and spend as much time as your child's interest allows to sign **WATER**. You can pour the water over their hands or over their toys while you sign it and have them sign it back to you. Of course, you should remain with them while playing with water for their safety.

Juice

✳ Memory Tip

It's as if you were drinking a beverage, and the *J* stands for *juice*.

✚ Similar Sign

This sign can be mixed up with **ORANGE** (page 58) since it is similar in handshape and placement.

✓ Signing Tip

You can sign **APPLE** (page 56), **GRAPE** (page 59), or **ORANGE** and then **JUICE** to specify the type of juice.

Hold your dominant hand in the ı handshape in front of your mouth, with the fist mimicking a cup. Sign a letter ᴊ twice quickly. You're not fully signing ᴊ but doing a short twisting motion of the pinkie.

Milk

With the dominant hand in a loose, open s handshape, squeeze it closed twice.

✱ Memory Tip

It's as if you were milking a cow but without the pulling motion.

✅ Signing Tip

This is fairly easy for kids to sign and a great one to introduce early, as your response to their request and the connection to the sign **MILK** will help them understand the significance of signing.

💡 Teaching Tip

This may be a favorite sign for your child if they love milk. Have them sign **MILK** when you pour them a cup of milk or pour it over their cereal. You can pull up a video of someone milking a cow and show them the motion of the person milking the cow and that the sign is very similar. Have them point to the stream of milk and sign **MILK**.

More

With both hands in a flat o handshape, touch the fingertips of each hand together twice in front of your body.

✳ Memory Tip

You are taking two objects and bringing them together to increase the amount you have.

💡 Teaching Tip

Have a simple snack that your child can eat a lot of without overdoing it, such as crackers or cereal pieces. Give them a cracker. Sign **MORE**, and hand them another cracker. Sign it again, and hand them another cracker. Have them sign **MORE**, and hand them another. This is a good sign to teach after you've taught the food sign for **CRACKER** (page 64) or **CEREAL** (page 69). Teach the sign for the food before you teach the sign **MORE**. Once they've caught on to what *more* is, you can sign **CRACKER MORE** or **CEREAL MORE**.

💝 ASD Tip

For children with ASD, this sign is best skipped until they've mastered requesting at least a dozen objects that they can both see and not see. Otherwise, they'll begin to sign **MORE** to represent any of these objects, and you both will wind up frustrated and confused.

Asking Questions

As we discussed in chapter 3, facial expressions are extremely important. In ASL we use facial expressions to ask questions. This is often the only way you know someone is asking a question rather than making a statement.

If you sign MILK (page 76) with a neutral facial expression, others know that you're merely bringing up the object. If you sign it with your eyebrows raised while leaning your head forward, others know you're asking a question about milk.

In ASL, you can ask questions in a variety of ways. Since you and your family are just beginning to learn sign language, the easiest and best way to begin is to use the eyebrow method.

You can sign any of the food signs in this chapter and merely raise your eyebrows to ask a question about it. If you sign FOOD (page 18) while raising your eyebrows, you are asking, "Do you want food?" If you sign a specific food item while raising your eyebrows, you are now asking if someone wants that specific food item.

Practice raising your eyebrows and making the rest of your face look as though it's asking a question. Now, use this expression when signing different food signs. Sign each sign both with a neutral facial expression and with your eyebrows raised.

This facial expression is used for yes-or-no questions only. If someone can respond with a *yes* or a *no* to the question you are asking, then use raised eyebrows and lean slightly forward.

Finish

Hold both hands in the 5 handshape just above your shoulders, and twist your hands back and forth.

✳ **Memory Tip**

You are holding your hands up after completing a task in a competition to show you are the first done.

💬 **Other Meaning**

You can use this sign for **FINISH**, **ALL DONE**, and **ALL GONE**; it's also used for **APPLAUSE**.

🔗 **Grammar Tip**

To make a sign or sentence past tense, sign **FINISH** and then either the remainder of the sentence or the sign it directly affects. For instance, to sign **DRANK**, you would sign **FINISH** and then **DRINK** (page 17).

Sign Practice

READ AND SIGN

Gather up some of your child's books that talk about food, and add some new ones from the library. They can be picture books that show different food items or stories about food. A few to get you started are *An Alphabet Salad* by Sarah L. Schuette, *Chicks and Salsa* by Aaron Reynolds, *Dragons Love Tacos* by Adam Rubin, and *Eating the Alphabet* by Lois Ehlert.

FRUIT SALAD

Gather up all the fruits you have learned in this chapter, and make a fruit salad together. Go to the grocery store together and pick them out, signing each as you add it to your cart. When you get home, sign the name of each fruit as you wash it. While you cut them, sign their names. As you put each into the bowl, sign the name. Mix in some flavored yogurt, signing YOGURT (page 70), of course, and have your child mix it all up. Eat your delicious fruit salad and sign as you find different fruits in your bowl.

SIGN AND SING

Sign this song to the tune of "I'm a Little Teapot." While you're singing, sign the signs you know, and for now, skip over the rest.

> *I'm a juicy orange, round as can be.*
> *A big, juicy orange, hanging on a tree.*
> *If you want some juice, just pick me.*
> *Poke in a straw and squeeze, squeeze,*
> *squeeze.*

You can find a lot of preschool fruit songs and videos on YouTube.

ASKING QUESTIONS

Practice signing a variety of signs, not just the food signs you've learned in this chapter, while raising your eyebrows to indicate a yes-or-no question. You will want to master this and demonstrate this concept to your child. As you sign CHEESE (page 71) and raise your eyebrows, you can ask, "Do you want cheese?" You can also use this same combination to ask, "Can I have cheese?"

If your child is signing something as a request, model how to ask with your facial expressions and sign. Help them raise their eyebrows as they sign it, and then hand them the object of their request. Sign YES back to them, and hand them the requested object once they have the idea down. Once the concept of asking questions by raising their eyebrows and signing the object is mastered, feel free to start denying requests when needed. Otherwise, you'll find yourself giving them candy at all hours of the day!

If your child with ASD is unable to form the "question" eyebrows, you can teach them how to sign the question-mark sign down the road. Your main goal right now is for them to master the signs and use them to communicate and make requests. As their language and communication skills develop, you can have them try again with the eyebrows, or have them sign a question mark with their index finger to indicate a request. Or they can use the sign PLEASE (page 123).

5

At Home

THESE SIGNS COVER some of the most common words and situations from your child's daily routine, and they will be a huge help in furthering your conversations. You and your child will be relieved to have many more signs to use to express yourselves and talk about the day-to-day things that come up regularly.

In chapter 2, you learned **BATHROOM** (page 25) and **HOME** (page 26), which accompany the signs in this chapter. You can use this as the perfect time to review those as you introduce these new signs.

All these signs are easily identifiable with objects or activities, such as **HOT** (page 90), **COLD** (page 91), **DIRTY** (page 87), and **CLEAN** (page 86), which means they are easier signs to teach to children with autism or to kids who are younger and struggle with more abstract concepts at this stage of their development.

Bed

With your dominant hand in a flat hand-shape, raise the palm to the side of your face while tilting your head.

✳ Memory Tip

It's as if you're resting your head on a pillow.

🧩 Similar Sign

This sign can be mixed up with **PILLOW**, which is a two-handed sign at the side of the face, as well.

🕊 Sign Variation

You may see this signed with both hands placed palm to palm and raised to the side of the face. Both variations are correct, but the one-handed version is easier and more modern.

Bath

With both hands in the s handshape, place them just below your collarbone and move them up and down on your chest two times.

It's like you're scrubbing with a washcloth.

Similar Sign

This sign can be mixed up with JACKET (page 98), which is signed with the same handshape and in the same location. BATH is an up-and-down movement, while JACKET is a downward-only movement.

Teaching Tip

Introduce this sign at bath time. Have your child help fill the tub with water, adding toys and bubbles if you have them. While you're running the water, demonstrate the sign a few times. Help them form the sign, as well. Once they're in the bath, sign it a few more times while your child plays.

Clean

With both hands in a flat handshape, hold your nondominant hand, palm up, in front of your body. Slide the palm of your dominant hand across the nondominant hand's palm two times. After the first slide, shift your hands slightly to the right (or to the left, if you're left-handed).

✳ **Memory Tip**

It's like wiping counters with a washcloth.

🧩 **Similar Sign**

This sign is very close to the sign NICE, but NICE is signed with one slide of the palm, while CLEAN is two slides. CLEAN is also similar to SCHOOL. SCHOOL uses a double clapping motion, and while it's not a lot like CLEAN, when CLEAN is signed quickly, it can take on a clapping look with the second slide. To avoid confusion, be sure to move the hands before you do the second slide.

💡 **Teaching Tip**

Three books your child will love to read that talk about cleaning are *Monster Mess* by Margery Cuyler, *How Do Dinosaurs Clean Their Rooms?* by Jane Yolen and Mark Teague, and *Just a Mess* by Mercer Mayer. You can read them together, and as the characters begin to clean, stop and practice the sign. Whenever the word *clean* is used in the story, or the character is cleaning in a picture, sign CLEAN. This sign is used for both picking up clutter and cleaning with rags.

Dirty

With your dominant hand in the 5 hand-shape, place the back of the hand underneath your chin with your fingers pointing to the side. Wiggle your fingers two or three times.

✳ Memory Tip

This sign is closely related to **PIG**, and pigs are often dirty.

❝❝ Other Meaning

You can also use this sign to mean **MESSY**.

✚❖ Similar Sign

This sign is similar to **PIG**. The fingers wiggle for the sign **DIRTY**, and for **PIG** they move up and down, bending at a 90-degree angle.

💡 Teaching Tip

This sign would be perfect to teach alongside **CLEAN** (page 86), especially if you use the books recommended. In the books there are ample opportunities to point out the dirty rooms and messes. You can point out the opposites and walk through your own home together, pointing out things that are dirty and things that are clean.

Clothes

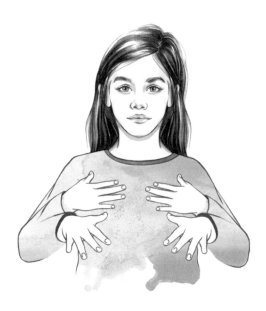

With both hands in the 5 handshape, thumbs just under the shoulders, brush them down the chest a bit, two times.

＊ Memory Tip

Think of fabric draped over the body.

✚ Similar Sign

This sign is similar to **DRESS**, which uses the same handshape and motion but is a longer movement, down to the waist.

💡 Teaching Tip

Have your child help you with the laundry, putting it into the washing machine or dryer, or putting all the clothes away, and sign **CLOTHES**.

Nonmanual Markers

A large part of ASL grammar is what we call *nonmanual markers*. These are important things we add to a sign to give it meaning that isn't communicated with our hands or arms. One form of a nonmanual marker that you have seen in these chapters is *mouth morphemes*. These are shapes your mouth makes to add meaning and clarity to a sign. For instance, when you sign **SCARED** (page 46), you clench your teeth. There are many mouth morphemes, but we'll go over three common ones.

The names of the mouth morphemes are the sounds you would make in order to form that shape. When using mouth morphemes, you don't actually make the sound—just make the shape.

OOO: Your lips purse together to say "ooo." You use this mouth morpheme for the sign **COLD** (page 91). This is also used when describing anything small.

MMM: Your lips are mashed together as if saying, "Mmm, that's interesting." Use this for a neutral facial expression, for describing medium-size things, or for other signs that specifically require it.

CHA: Your mouth will open up when you form this mouth morpheme. The *CH* is formed similar to *cha-cha*, but if you were to say the sound, it would sound more like "chu" in *chug*. This mouth morpheme is used for anything large, tall, or big.

ASD Tip

For children with ASD, nonmanual markers are an advanced concept. In fact, they may not develop these morphemes for years or at all. Although you should use them and encourage their use when appropriate, children with ASD can still express themselves without using them. As the person who knows your child's abilities best, you'll know when it's time to push them and when to back off.

Hot

Place your dominant hand in a bent 5 handshape facing your mouth like a breathing mask, and twist it away from your face.

☺ **Nonmanual Marker**

When signing **HOT**, be sure to have your mouth open, as if you're saying "Ha."

✳ **Memory Tip**

It's as if the air is too hot near your face and you have to turn it away.

✠ **Similar Sign**

This sign is similar to **WARM** and **ANGRY** (page 48). **WARM** is an upward movement and doesn't twist away. **ANGRY** stays in front of the mouth and the fingers bend twice.

Cold

Hold both hands in the s handshape in front of your shoulders. Shake your hands slightly, side to side, a few times.

 Nonmanual Marker

Purse your lips together, as if you were whistling, when you sign **COLD**.

 Memory Tip

You're shivering in the cold.

 Teaching Tip

Give your child a cup of ice water. This sign is more confusing to teach with only water or only ice. Put your hand in the cup of ice water, pull it out quickly, and sign **COLD**. Put your hand in again and sign it again. Have your child put their hand in the cup, and sign **COLD**. Now, teach them how to sign it, as well. If you have access to other cold items, such as snow or ice packs, use them to further teach this concept.

Brush teeth

Wiggle the index finger of your dominant hand up and down and across your exposed teeth.

🙂 **Nonmanual Marker**

It's important to have your teeth exposed. You do this by clenching your teeth and pulling back your lips.

✳ **Memory Tip**

It looks like you're brushing your teeth.

🧩 **Similar Sign**

This sign is somewhat similar to **CEREAL** (page 69). You probably won't confuse how to sign **BRUSH TEETH** since it's intuitive, but it is not uncommon to mix up the signs **CEREAL** and **BRUSH TEETH** when wanting to sign **CEREAL**, or seeing it signed, since the only difference is placement around the mouth. These two signs may be confused by your child or look very similar to one another as they sign them.

Blanket

 Memory Tip

It looks as though you're pulling up a blanket to cover yourself.

Similar Sign

BLANKET is very similar to JACKET (page 98). JACKET starts from the shoulders and moves down, while BLANKET starts on the chest and moves up to the shoulder.

Teaching Tip

For family time, grab a big blanket and have each person gather a corner and raise it up and down together, like a parachute. You can sit underneath it as it covers you. Another game is to place stuffed animals in the center of it and throw them up and down with the blanket. When you pull out the blanket, sign BLANKET a few times, and then sign it a few more times during the game.

With both hands in the s handshape, starting from your chest, pull your hands up and out to your shoulders. Your hands will make small arcs and will slide up your chest.

Book

Hold both hands in a flat handshape in front of your body with your palms together. Keeping the pinkies touching, open and close your hands quickly, two times.

✳ Memory Tip

It looks like a book opening and closing.

◖ Similar Sign

This sign can be mixed up with the sign for **BOAT**. **BOAT** stays in the open position and is curved, but the two signs can look similar when signed quickly or with younger hands that struggle to form signs fully.

↳ Sign Variation

You can turn this sign into a verb by changing the movement. If you open and close your hands in rapid succession, twice, it is the noun **BOOK**. If you open your hands all the way, so that both palms are facing up, and leave them open, you have now signed **OPEN BOOK**. If you take your open hands and bring the palms together, you are now signing **CLOSE BOOK**. Any type of message that you want to communicate that includes opening or closing a book would use these variations on the sign **BOOK**.

Shirt

Using your dominant hand in the F handshape, pinch the front of your shirt and pull twice. You'll want to pinch off-center, closest to your dominant hand, and not dead center.

✳ Memory Tip
You're showing your shirt.

▪ Similar Sign
This sign for **SHIRT** is nearly identical to the sign for **VOLUNTEER**. **VOLUNTEER** is often signed with an upward-pulling motion to make it clearer, along with raised eyebrows. Context clues will be the best way to differentiate. You can also sign **SHIRT** with both hands doing the same motion simultaneously.

✅ Signing Tip
This sign is used for a variety of shirt types. If you need to specify, sign **SHIRT** and then fingerspell the name of the shirt type. If you do not have a shirt on while signing this, pinch just in front of your body and pretend to pull as if you had fabric in your hand.

Skirt

Start with both hands in the 5 handshape at the waist. Flare your hands out in a downward motion.

* Memory Tip

It looks as though you're pulling up your pants.

❞ Other Meaning

You can use this sign for all types of pants, like **JEANS** or **SLACKS**.

✛ Similar Sign

You sign **PANTS** similarly enough to **SKIRT** that the two signs may get mixed up. **PANTS** is with both hands in the **4** handshape starting at the top of your thighs. From there, pull your hands up to your waistband into a flat **O** handshape twice. **SKIRT** is signed by flaring your hands out.

Shoes

Think of two shoes clicking together, like Dorothy's in *The Wizard of Oz*.

🧩 Similar Sign

This sign is similar to the sign **WITH**. It's not so similar that they look the same, but they are often mixed up with one another. **WITH** brings the knuckles of both hands together in front of the body. It's the coming together motion in a fist shape that often throws people.

✓ Signing Tip

The sign **SHOES** can be used for all varieties of footwear. If you want to specify the type, you would sign **SHOES** and then fingerspell the type of shoe.

With both hands in the s handshape, bring them in front of your body and tap the thumb sides of your hands together, twice.

Jacket

Holding both hands in the s handshape, drag them down your body from your shoulders to your chest. The motion will be a slight arc.

✳ Memory Tip
It looks as though you were putting on your jacket.

🗝 Other Meaning
You use this sign for **JACKET**, **COAT**, **PARKA**, **TUNIC**, and **BLAZER**.

🧩 Similar Sign
JACKET looks very similar to **BLANKET** (page 93). **BLANKET** moves up the body, while **JACKET** moves down.

Dog

 Sign Variation

There are a few ways to sign **DOG** that you may see. Some people pat the side of their leg, and others may pat their leg and snap their fingers together. The most modern version of this sign is the abbreviated snap version here.

 ASD Tip

If your child has trouble moving their fingers in the snap formation, teach them the leg-pat version.

With your dominant hand in the κ hand-shape held out in front of you, wiggle your middle finger against your thumb back and forth as if you were snapping quickly.

✳ Memory Tip

It looks as though you are snapping your fingers to get the dog's attention.

Cat

With your dominant hand in the F hand-shape, bring the fingertips of your thumb and index finger from the side of your mouth outward to the side.

✱ Memory Tip

The three extended fingers of the F hand look like cat whiskers.

🔁 Sign Variation

You may see people sign this with both hands instead of just the dominant hand.

💡 Teaching Tip

Show your child pictures of cats and kittens to teach them this sign. If you have a cat, or access to a cat, have your child pet the cat as you teach the sign.

Door

Hold both hands in the B handshape in front of your body with palms facing out, fingers pointing up, and index fingers touching. Bring your dominant hand backward toward your body. This is a hinging movement, so the pinkie side of your hand will stay in the same location while the thumb side will open up toward your body. Do this movement twice.

✴ Memory Tip

It looks just like a door opening and closing.

🛫 Sign Variation

Just as with the sign for **BOOK** (page 94), you can make **DOOR** into an action sign. If you do the movement only once (and make the movement a bit bigger) and hold it, you are signing **OPEN DOOR**. If you begin from the "open" position and put the hands together, you are signing **CLOSE DOOR**.

💡 Teaching Tip

Walk through your house pointing to all the doors. Sign **DOOR** and then move to the next door and sign it again. Sign together for each door in the house. You can then practice signing **OPEN DOOR** and **CLOSE DOOR**.

Window

Hold both hands in the B handshape in front of your body with palms facing you, fingers pointing sideways in opposite directions, and your dominant hand on top of the nondominant hand. The pinkie of your dominant hand should be on top of the index finger of your nondominant hand. Bring your dominant hand up and down twice.

✳ Memory Tip

It looks as if you are opening and closing a window.

🔁 Sign Variation

You can also make **WINDOW** into an action sign. If you do the movement only once and hold it, you are signing **OPEN WINDOW**. If you begin from the "open" position and put the hands together, you are signing **CLOSE WINDOW**.

💡 Teaching Tip

Make teaching this sign fun by gathering window clings, window stickers, or window markers. Decorate your windows together to introduce the sign, and enjoy yourselves.

Sign Practice

CLOTHES SORTING

Head to your child's closet and pick out several outfits' worth of clothes and shoes. Lift an item of clothing, and have your child sign its name. Sort them into piles: pants, shirts, and so on.

Once they're all sorted, put together complete outfits from the piles you've created, with each having a shirt, pants, and shoes. You can sign the name of each clothing item as you place the outfits together, or you can point to each item in the assembled outfits and sign it.

NOUNS TO VERBS

You'll need three things for this activity: a book, a door, and a window that opens and closes. Practice the sign for each item first.

Open the book, and demonstrate the sign for **OPEN BOOK**, as found in the Sign Variations for the sign **BOOK** (page 94). Close the book, and sign **CLOSE BOOK**. Open it again, and have your child sign after you. Close the book, and sign it with your child. Do the same with the **WINDOW** (page 102) and the **DOOR** (page 101). After you've introduced the concept, go back and forth with the objects, quizzing your child.

Variation 1: Open the door, close the window, and open the book, and have your child sign each matching action sign.

Variation 2: Sign one action sign, and have your child complete the action with the right object and action. For instance, when you sign **CLOSE DOOR**, they would close the door.

NONMANUAL MARKERS

Pull out paper and markers, and together draw various sizes of dogs and cats. Draw a big dog, a tiny dog, and a medium-size dog. Do the same with the cats. Exaggerate their sizes to be as obvious as you can.

Practice the signs **DOG** (page 99) and **CAT** (page 100), and then point to the individual animals. Use your hands to show if it's big, medium, or tiny, bringing them wide for big (or sign **BIG**, page 126), about a foot apart for medium, and really close together for small (or sign **LITTLE**, page 127). Use your index finger and thumb to show if it's really tiny. When you are demonstrating *big*, do the CHA mouth morpheme, MMM when it's medium, and OOO when it's small.

Do this a few times on your own before prompting your child to do the same with their hands and mouth. You may have to demonstrate just the mouth morphemes first before adding the hands.

Point to the different-size dogs and cats until your child has mastered the concept or grows bored. You can come back to this activity later using different objects that you find in books or around the house.

6

Playtime

LEARNING PLAYTIME SIGNS will be an enjoyable treat. What kid doesn't want to play just a little longer? The signs in this chapter should be learned fairly easily due to kids' higher motivation to learn and use the signs.

Many of the signs you've learned so far can be used in conjunction with these signs. You can use **YES** (page 27) and **NO** (page 28) signs to ask questions. You can use emotion signs to gauge how they're feeling. Maybe they are **SCARED** (page 46) by something outside, or you can see them smiling and laughing and sign **HAPPY** (page 43). Or you could bring a picnic to the park and sign about the foods you brought.

Friend

With both hands in the x handshape in front of your body, hook the two xs together, with the dominant hand on top, then switch so that the nondominant hand is on top.

✳ Memory Tip

It's like two people coming together with a tight hug.

🐾 Sign Variation

One way to vary the sign to show that you are really good friends, or best friends, is to link both **x** fingers together and, instead of switching hands, hold them up and pull against the fingers. It winds up being a bit of a shaking motion, but it shows that you're "really tight." Another way to sign **BEST FRIEND** is to hold the **R** handshape up, palm facing your body, and do a strong tap in the air toward the other person.

💡 Teaching Tip

Use picture books, storybooks, TV shows, and pictures of your child with their actual friends to teach this sign. When they have the chance to play with other kids, make a point to sign **FRIEND** with them several times to help them make the connection between pictures and real life.

Play

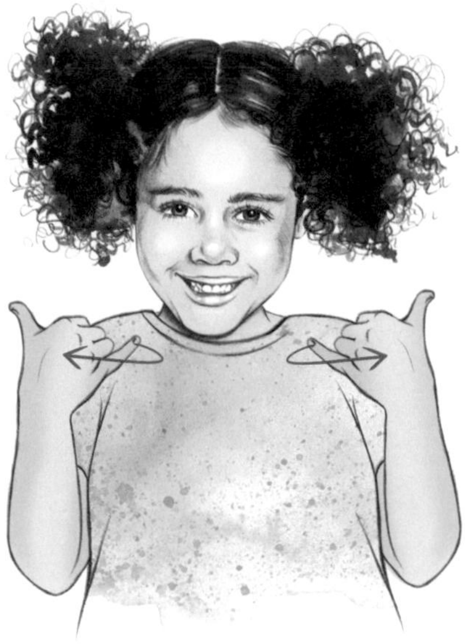

Hold both hands in the Y handshape in front of your body with palms facing each other, then flick/fling your wrists so that your palms face down. This motion is done twice.

✱ Memory Tip

The flinging **Y**s are bouncy and lively, just like a kid who's playing.

Similar Sign

PARTY is similar to **PLAY**, in that it has the same handshape and location, but the movement is slightly different. Instead of moving in opposite directions, for **PARTY**, the hands move side to side in a swinging motion in tandem.

Sign Variation

To emphasize that you were playing a lot or that there were a lot of people playing, you can sign **PLAY** with a fun twist: Sign **PLAY** with your hands shifted to the right of your body, then out in front of your body on the right side, then shifted to the left, and then one last time closer to the left of your body. When you do this, you do one flicking motion per hand position instead of two. Your hands are a bit farther from the body than normal, and you're drawing a rectangle in front of your body with the four points.

Outside

With your dominant hand in a loose c handshape, with the hand at head level and your palm facing you, pull your hand out away from your head, bringing the fingers together to form a flat o hand-shape. Do this short pulling motion twice.

✳ Memory Tip

You're pulling yourself from the inside to the outside of the building.

⤲ Sign Variation

You can sign this once, with a stern face, to tell your child to **GO OUT**, whether you mean outside or out of the room.

✅ Signing Tip

Don't confuse this with the sign for **OUT**. Use **OUT** in statements such as "I pulled the hat out of the box." Sign **OUT** with your dominant hand in a flat **o** handshape, tucked inside your nondominant hand, which is in the **c** handshape, by pulling the dominant hand out of the other hand.

Rain

Your fingers are drops of rain falling from the sky.

✜ **Similar Sign**

This sign is similar to **SNOW**, which has the same handshape and location, but instead of the fingers coming down in straight lines, to sign **SNOW**, you slightly wiggle the fingers and sway them side to side as they move down.

➤ **Sign Variation**

You can change the way you sign **RAIN** to demonstrate different types of rain. For instance, to indicate a **LIGHT RAIN**, you can sign this with smaller and shorter movements while using the OOO nonmanual marker. If you want to show a heavier rain, use the CHA nonmanual marker and make your movements bigger and stronger, and move the hands down further. You can change the direction the rain is coming in by changing the angle and starting location of your hands, as well. Signing this way is what makes ASL a lot of fun.

Hold both your hands in the 5 handshape with palms facing away from you at a 45-degree angle just above or at head level. Bring the fingertips down in a short movement so that the palms are facing down. Raise the fingertips again, then lower your fingertips one more time.

Sun

With your dominant hand in the c hand-shape, with the thumb resting on the bone just below your eye, raise your hand up and to the right (or to the left, if you're left-handed) to a spot in the sky.

✳ Memory Tip

You can remember this by saying, "I C the sun in the sky."

✚ Similar Sign

MOON is very close to this sign. Everything is the same except for the handshape, which is like the c shape but made only with the index finger and thumb.

➴ Sign Variation

There is another, equally acceptable version of this sign. Start with your dominant hand in a flat o handshape above and to the right (or to the left, if you're left-handed) of your head. Circle the wrist once and then open your hand into a bell shape with the fingers pointing down toward your head, like sun rays. It's important to know both, and you may find one is easier for your child to sign than the other.

Tree

✳ Memory Tip

The nondominant arm represents the ground, the dominant arm is the tree trunk, and the fingers are its branches.

✜ Similar Sign

This sign is very similar to **FOREST**. **FOREST** is made by signing **TREE** and moving your arms in an arc toward your body while continuously twisting the dominant hand.

✔ Signing Tip

Use **TREE** to describe all types of trees, including Christmas trees and palm trees. To specify the type of tree, sign **TREE** and then fingerspell the name, for instance, **TREE O-A-K**.

Hold your nondominant hand in a flat handshape in front of your body with the palm facing down. Place the elbow of your dominant arm on top of the back of the nondominant hand. With your dominant hand in the 5 handshape, twist the hand back and forth a few times.

Flower

With your dominant hand in a flat o handshape, place the fingertips on the nostril on the same side as your dominant hand and then arc over the bridge of the nose and touch the other nostril.

✳ **Memory Tip**

This sign references smelling flowers.

✅ **Signing Tip**

Use **FLOWER** to describe all types of flowers, such as tulips and daffodils. To specify the type of flower, you sign **FLOWER** and then fingerspell the name, for instance, **FLOWER P-A-N-S-Y**. You may see some people sign **ROSE** by signing **FLOWER** with the **R** handshape, but this version isn't as widely accepted or recognized as it used to be.

💡 **Teaching Tip**

Take your child on a tour of your garden, the flower shop, a garden center, or a farmers' market. If there aren't any flowers around you, use a picture book. Instruct your child to pick out (or point to) flowers, smell them, and together appreciate their beauty as you practice signing **FLOWER**.

Doll

With your dominant hand in the x hand-shape, place the index finger on the bridge of your nose and drag it down to the tip of the nose, two times.

✳ Memory Tip

This is admittedly a strange sign. It's closely related to the sign FAKE, and dolls are fake (or pretend) people.

❞ Other Meaning

Your child can use this sign to describe any dolls they may play with, including baby dolls, action figures, 18-inch dolls, and all types to be found.

🧩 Similar Sign

There are three signs that use the **x** handshape and are signed at the nose: DOLL, WITCH, and EAGLE. WITCH starts on the side of the nose and is curved forward and out, like a witch's big nose. EAGLE is signed with the back of the index finger tapping the length of the nose twice.

Share

Start with both hands in a flat hand-shape, with the thumbs extended. Hold your nondominant hand out in front of your body, as if you were about to shake someone's hand. Place your dominant hand, palm facing you, on the index finger of your nondominant hand and slide it along the index finger, back and forth, twice.

✳ Memory Tip

It's as if you're passing something back and forth between two people.

🧩 Similar Sign

This sign can be mixed up with the sign for **ANNOY**. **ANNOY** uses a tapping motion on the nondominant hand instead of a sliding motion.

💔 ASD Tip

This concept may be tricky for your child to understand right away. Make sure they understand what sharing means before teaching the sign. If they haven't yet mastered a dozen object request signs, put off teaching this sign until they do. If your child is familiar with the concept, then teach the sign while going through this chapter.

Jump

✳ Memory Tip

It's like your legs jumping off the ground.

Sign Variation

You can show the amount of jumping, the height of the jump, and the type of jumping by varying the way you have your "legs" jump when signing. You can even show jumping on one leg. Play around with different types of jumping.

💡 Teaching Tip

Have fun by jumping around with your child. You can jump onto pieces of paper, off a step, or around the yard. If your child is unable to jump, you can watch a video of animals jumping around. Demonstrate the sign and jump, then sign again and jump. Have your child sign and jump, too.

With your nondominant hand held palm up, in a flat handshape, make a 2 hand-shape with your dominant hand and place the fingertips on the nondominant palm. Bend the fingers a bit and have them "jump" off the palm and land back down again.

Run

✳ Memory Tip

This is one of those weird signs, but you can think of the thumbs sticking up as legs and the index fingers as feet.

🧩 Similar Sign

RUN is similar to FAST. With FAST, your hands are not hooked together; instead, both index fingers bend simultaneously as the hands kick up.

🦋 Sign Variation

You can show someone is running fast, or intensely, by moving your hands forward slowly as you bend your dominant index finger. When you do this sign, puff your cheeks out to show the intensity of the sign.

With both of your hands in the L hand-shape and held horizontally in front of your body, palms facing sideways, point away from your body at an angle. Hook the index finger of the nondominant hand around the thumb of the dominant hand and bend the index finger of the dominant hand two times.

Ball

With both hands in a curved 5 hand-shape and held in front of the body, tap the fingertips together twice.

 Memory Tip

The sign shows the shape of a ball.

Teaching Tip

Bring out a ball or several of them of all sizes and types. Play together while you introduce the sign to your child. Sit across from each other on the floor. Line up all the balls in front of your child. Sign the size of ball you want your child to roll to you. Sign **BALL** with your hands close together to show a small ball; hold your hands farther apart, making the tapping movement without having your fingers touch, to show a medium-sized ball; and hold your hands out wide and do the same motion to show a larger ball. You can practice the Nonmanual Markers (page 103) you learned in chapter 5, too. For large, use CHA; for medium, use MMM; and for small, use OOO. If they roll the wrong size, walk it back over and have them try again. After they've rolled all the balls to you, it's their turn to sign to you as you roll the balls.

Playtime Interactions

You may find yourself worrying about what to do when your child is playing with other kids. How will they communicate? What do you do to prepare your child?

Do your best to take deep breaths and let go of the anxiety and worry about social situations. You can set up a playdate with friends you are both comfortable with at first, such as a play group, or head to the park.

When a kid begins to talk to your child, simply tell them the minimal amount of information they need. If your child has hearing loss, you can explain that your child cannot hear them speak but instead speaks with their hands and loves to play. You can offer to show them a sign or two, or demonstrate how you sign with each other.

If your child has ASD and is nonverbal, you can explain that your child hears and understands them but prefers to speak using their hands instead of their voice. You can teach a sign that fits the situation best.

You can also talk to the parents of the other kids and explain. Encourage them to allow their children to interact with yours. Explain how you and your child best enjoy interactions. Kids will figure out how to communicate with your child while playing together. The other kid may start to ask your child how to sign things, or your kid will naturally become the teacher and show them how to sign.

Sign Practice

SEE AND SIGN

Head to your favorite local park and do a mini scavenger hunt to find all the items you've learned in this chapter and any that you may find from previous chapters. See how many of the signs your child remembers. Practice the ones that have been forgotten, and correct inaccurate signs.

SIGN A STORY

At your library, check out the books *Please Take Me for a Walk* by Susan Gal and *Go, Bikes, Go!* by Addie Boswell. *Go, Bikes, Go!* not only talks about the outdoors but depicts various sizes of bikes with which you can practice your nonmanual markers for showing size. You can sign BIKE by holding out two S hands in front of your body and circle them around just as if you were pedaling a bike.

As you read the book, point out pictures or words that match the signs you've learned from this chapter and the previous chapters, as well. Prompt your child to sign as you point to the images.

CONNECT THE SIGNS

Begin to put signs together in phrases. Don't worry about full sentences at this stage. Right now we're focusing on learning signs and on beginning to combine two signs together for a more complete thought.

For instance, you can sign OUTSIDE (page 108) and HOT (page 90) to say it's hot outside. If you raise your eyebrows while signing the same phrase, you're now asking, "Is it hot outside?" Find easy combinations that make sense to practice putting together, and then practice making it a question. You can turn it into a fun game.

You can ask OUTSIDE HOT? Your child can then answer YES (page 27) or NO (page 28), and if they're able, they could respond NO, it's COLD (page 91).

Try combining other signs, like BABY (page 39), DOG (page 99), CAT (page 100), SISTER (page 37), and BROTHER (page 38), with emotions, and you can include sizes, as well.

7

Everyday Conversation

THIS CHAPTER TEACHES signs that you'll use every single day. As you further your conversational skills, you'll begin to feel like you are all communicating with one another in a very real way. These signs make especially useful complements to the ones you learned in chapters 2 and 5, but they can be combined with many of the signs throughout the book to create phrases and sentences.

Thank you

Place the fingertips of your dominant hand, in a flat handshape, at the tip of your chin. Bring your hand down to a 45-degree angle.

✳ **Memory Tip**

This sign looks like you're blowing someone a kiss.

❞ **Other Meaning**

You can sign **THANK YOU** to mean **GRATEFUL**, **GRATITUDE**, **PLEASED**, and **THANKS**.

✖ **Similar Sign**

This sign is similar to **GOOD**, which you will learn later in this chapter. The difference is that for **GOOD**, the hand lands on the palm of the nondominant hand.

Please

With your dominant hand in a flat hand-shape, place it on your chest and make a small circle twice, starting in a downward motion.

✳ Memory Tip

It's like putting your hand to your heart to plead with someone.

🧩 Similar Sign

PLEASE is similar to ENJOY. ENJOY is signed with both hands, with the dominant hand on the chest and the nondominant hand on the stomach.

💔 ASD Tip

You may want to delay teaching signs about manners to your child with ASD, as they can be hard concepts to grasp. They may sign PLEASE when they really mean to name an object. Be sure they have mastered requesting objects before introducing this sign.

Like

Start with your dominant hand in the 5 handshape in front of your chest, with the palm facing your body. Pull your hand away from your chest while bringing your thumb and middle finger together.

 Memory Tip

You're pulling an object from your heart.

Similar Sign

LIKE is very similar to a variation of **INTERESTING**. That sign is done with both hands, with the dominant hand starting in front of the face and the nondominant hand starting in front of the stomach. The handshapes and movement are the same.

Teaching Tip

To teach the signs **LIKE** and **DON'T LIKE** (page 125), make a pile of several food items or pictures of food that you know your child has an opinion about. Go through the items or pictures, and ask your child if they like or don't like one of the food items. Have them answer with the sign **LIKE** or **DON'T LIKE**. You can do this with a variety of objects. Have them sort the objects into piles, and encourage them to use matching facial expressions when signing.

Don't like

First, create the sign for LIKE (page 124), and as you pull away from your chest with the middle finger and thumb coming together, twist your wrist away from your body and flick your middle finger.

It's important to show a negative expression when signing this sign. You can shake your head, curl your lip, purse your lips in disapproval, or do another variation of negating with your face.

✳ **Memory Tip**

You are flicking something away from you in disgust.

✅ **Signing Tip**

LIKE and **DON'T LIKE** are very similar to one another, but **DON'T LIKE** is the negative version, being flicked away from the body. This method is used for several signs to negate the positive version. You'll see this method for the signs GOOD (page 142) and BAD (page 143) later in this chapter.

Big

☺ **Nonmanual Marker**

Use the CHA mouth morpheme when signing **BIG**.

✳ **Memory Tip**

Your hands are indicating the bigness of an object.

✅ **Signing Tip**

You would not use this sign to show that something is tall. To sign **TALL** or **BIG IN HEIGHT**, you would instead hold your dominant hand vertically in front of you with the fingers bent at a 90-degree angle so the backs of the fingers are facing up. With this handshape, bring your hand just above your head and then raise it up higher, using the CHA mouth morpheme at the same time.

With both hands in a curved L handshape in front of your body with palms facing each other, move your hands out away from each other.

Little

Start with both hands in a flat handshape in front of you with the palms facing each other, and bring your hands close to one another.

Use the OOO mouth morpheme when signing **LITTLE**.

✳ **Memory Tip**

Your hands are showing how small something is.

🗩 **Other Meaning**

This sign can also be used for **SMALL**, **TINY**, and **MINIATURE**. Using the mouth morpheme will add to your meaning to show the intended size. The smaller the object, the more pursed your OOO should be.

Hungry

Your hand is tracing down your esophagus into your empty stomach.

Similar Sign

HUNGRY is very close to the sign WISH, except WISH stops at the top of the chest, whereas HUNGRY stops at the top of the stomach. It is important that you sign both of these signs using only one movement; never go up and down repeatedly.

Sign Variation

To say that you're STARVING, drag your hand down to your stomach slowly and in an exaggerated manner while also pairing it with a matching facial expression that shows you're super hungry.

With your dominant hand in the c handshape, place the tips of your fingers and thumb on your collarbone and drag them straight down your chest, stopping at the top of the stomach.

How

☺ **Nonmanual Marker**

HOW is a "wh-question" sign and is often paired with a mouth morpheme that has the lip pulled back or mouth open as if saying "Huh?" The brows must be furrowed and head tilted.

✳ **Memory Tip**

The hand turns out toward the other person to invite them to fill that empty cup with knowledge that the signer doesn't have.

🖐 **Sign Variation**

You might see this sign done two-handed, with both hands twisting so both palms are facing up and the fingertips are still touching. The one-handed version is more efficient and up-to-date.

Hold both hands in the c handshape with the thumbs sticking up and bring them to meet in front of the middle of the body with the palms facing you. Twist the dominant hand so that the palm is now facing up.

What

With both hands in a loose 5 handshape with palms facing up, shake both hands side to side, in front of the body, in opposite directions.

☺ **Nonmanual Marker**

WHAT is a wh-question sign. The brows must be furrowed and head tilted. If you sign the **W-T** version (see Sign Variation), you must look confounded or upset, as this is the outraged form of the sign. Your mouth should form the morpheme WHA, as if you were saying the first part of the word *what*.

✳ **Memory Tip**

This is a natural way to shrug your shoulders and ask, "Huh?"

🖐 **Sign Variation**

There are a few ways to sign **WHAT**. You can sign it as described above, or do the same but with one hand. You might also see this signed with the dominant hand drawing a line down the palm of the nondominant hand. A fourth version is done by quickly signing the letters **W** and **T**.

Why

😊 **Nonmanual Marker**

Your eyebrows should be furrowed and your head tilted forward like a lean, rather than looking at the floor. Form the mouth morpheme WHA, as if you were saying the first part of the word *what*. It is the same mouth morpheme as for the sign **WHAT** (page 130).

✳ **Memory Tip**

The movement of your finger indicates that your brain is trying to figure something out but can't quite grasp the answer.

🔁 **Sign Variation**

Another equally used version of this sign is to hold your hand in a flat handshape with the thumb extended near the temple, then pull down at a 45-degree angle into the **Y** handshape.

With your dominant hand is the 5 hand-shape at the side of the forehead near the temple, wiggle your middle finger up and down a few times.

What's your name?

You are signing three separate signs to make this sentence, in this order: YOUR, NAME, WHAT (page 130)?

To make the sign YOUR, place your dominant hand in a flat handshape directed toward the person you are speaking to. Your hand is at a 45-degree angle, and it's a short movement forward toward their body.

NAME is made with both hands in the H handshape. Cross the dominant hand over the nondominant hand, creating an X shape, with both hands held horizontally. Using the dominant hand, tap the bigger knuckle of the nondominant hand twice.

WHAT is signed with both hands in a loose 5 handshape, palms facing up. Shake both hands side to side, in front of the body, in opposite directions.

😊 **Nonmanual Marker**

As you sign WHAT, the eyebrows must be furrowed and the lips pulled back like you just said, "What?"

✳ **Memory Tip**

Possession (like YOUR) is shown with a flat palm. NAME makes an X shape with your crossed fingers, as in "Sign your name at the X."

🐾 **Sign Variation**

You can also ask this same question by signing NAME YOU? If you sign this version, be sure to raise your eyebrows while signing both signs.

My name is . . .

In this phrase, you will combine the signs for MY and NAME (see page 132):

Sign MY by placing the flat palm of your dominant hand on your chest.

NAME is made by both hands in the H handshape. Cross the dominant hand over the nondominant hand, creating an X shape, with both hands held horizontally. Using the dominant hand, tap the bigger knuckle of the nondominant hand twice.

After you sign MY NAME, fingerspell your name using the ASL alphabet in chapter 8 (page 147). You do not sign the word is.

✴ **Memory Tip**

MY is the possessive sign for ME. You are bringing something to your chest as if you were bringing the object closer to your body.

🔁 **Sign Variation**

Some people will point to themselves to sign I NAME rather than MY NAME. Both are acceptable and mean the same thing.

💡 **Teaching Tip**

Learning to fingerspell may take some time. If your child has a longer name, you can teach them a shortened version, or nickname, if they find that easier. To help you with fingerspelling, I have included Sign Practice activities in chapter 8 (page 155).

What's the sign for . . . ?

To ask this question, you will sign HOW (page 129) and SIGN:

To sign HOW, hold both hands in the c handshape with the thumbs sticking up and bring them to meet in front of the middle of the body with the palms facing you. Twist the dominant hand so that the palm is now facing up.

For SIGN, start with both your hands in the 1 handshape, held in front of the body, palms facing down. Move your hands simultaneously in alternating circles toward your body, with the dominant hand at an angle and higher up; the nondominant hand is also held at an angle below the dominant hand. The circles are small and done twice.

After you sign HOW SIGN, you then finger-spell the word you want to know the sign for.

☺ Nonmanual Marker

When asking this question, furrow your eyebrows and tilt forward.

✳ Memory Tip

SIGN shows the hands moving quickly as if signing to another person.

✅ Signing Tip

You'll be signing this a lot as you are learning ASL. This is a normal part of Deaf culture, as signs are always evolving and new ones are added or updated. Don't worry about asking this question frequently. After you fingerspell the word you want to learn, you can sign HOW again for added emphasis. The person you ask will respond with one of three options: the actual sign, they may say they don't know, or they will tell you to fingerspell the word because it doesn't have a sign.

Deaf

With your dominant hand in the 1 hand-shape, place the tip of the index finger at the corner of the mouth and then, in a small arc, move it to tap just in front of the ear, at the cheekbone.

✳ Memory Tip

This sign was first created to say that the person could neither speak nor hear, even though that's not always the case.

🧩 Similar Sign

This sign is similar to HOME (page 26). HOME is signed with a flat O handshape rather than the 1 handshape.

💨 Sign Variation

You will also see this sign start from the ear and arc down to the mouth. They are both the same sign. It is often done this way when the last sign used just before DEAF makes it more convenient to start at the ear rather than the mouth. It can also be used this way because of a person's preference for emphasizing the hearing portion of the sign rather than the mouth.

Hearing

With your dominant hand in the 1 hand-shape held horizontally with the palm facing toward the body, place the hand in front of your mouth and circle it out in a very small circle twice.

✳ Memory Tip

The finger circling represents words spilling out of the person's mouth.

⊹ Similar Sign

This sign can be confused with both **SAY** and **TELL**. **SAY** is signed by tapping the chin twice with the index finger, and **TELL** is signed by bringing the index finger out from the chin, similar in movement to the sign **THANK YOU** (page 122) using only the index finger.

✓ Signing Tip

This sign is in reference to a person's hearing status, not whether they are hearing you speak during a specific moment, nor is it a command to hear or listen to you. To ask if they can hear you, you would tap at your ear with your index finger and raise your eyebrows in a question.

Stop

With both hands in a flat handshape with the thumbs extended, hold the nondominant hand in front of your body with the palm up. Hold out your dominant hand as if you were about to shake someone's hand. Drop the dominant hand into the palm of the nondominant hand. It's a sharp, abrupt movement, not a mere tap.

✳ **Memory Tip**

The movement of this sign indicates that whatever is happening should end immediately. It cuts off the movement with its sharp drop.

🧩 **Similar Sign**

This sign is similar to **TACO** (page 63). The only difference is when signing **TACO**, the nondominant hand is bent to form a "taco shell." The dominant hand drops down into the shell using the same movement.

🔄 **Sign Variation**

You can use a variation of the sign **FINISH** (page 79) to say the same thing. This is especially useful when you need your child to immediately stop an action or behavior. Sign **FINISH**, one-handed, with the fingertips of the dominant hand pointing toward the person. You do the shaking movement once, and quite abruptly, to show the emotion behind the strong command.

Go

Hold both index fingers in front of your body, angled toward the dominant-hand side, with the dominant hand in front and the nondominant hand slightly behind it. Start with the index fingers pointed up, then drop your hands down sharply so the palms are facing down.

✳ Memory Tip

You are pointing with both fingers to indicate forward movement.

✚ Similar Sign

This sign is quite similar to **ANSWER**. To sign **ANSWER**, you do the same movement and handshape, but you have your nondominant hand start with the fingernail of the index finger touching the chin.

✈ Sign Variation

To sign **COME**, the opposite of **GO**, flip your hands so the palms are facing your body, then bend your hands down so your palms are facing down.

Autistic

✳ **Memory Tip**

The movement of the hand going into the pocket shows the containment of the autism and the self.

🟦 **Other Meaning**

This sign means **AUTISM** or **AUTISTIC** only in context. The other meanings for this sign are negative, but when it is used for **AUTISM** or **AUTISTIC**, it is not negative at all. The other meanings are **SELF-INVOLVED**, **SELF-ABSORBED**, and **IN YOUR OWN WORLD**.

🔁 **Sign Variation**

There are a few different ways to sign **AUTISM**. One is not as clear in the meaning, and the other is negative. The first is by holding the dominant hand in the **A** handshape at the side of the head and twisting the hand twice. The second is done by touching the head with the index finger (the sign for **THINK**), and then bringing both hands in a flat handshape from the sides of the eyes (like horse blinders) to in front of the face at an angle. Together, these signs mean **NARROW FOCUS**.

Hold your nondominant hand in the c handshape with fingertips and thumb touching the chest, forming a pocket. Starting with your dominant hand in a loose 5 handshape, move it into the pocket at the chest and close it into a flat o handshape. Both palms should be facing toward the body at the start. Once the dominant hand is in the "pocket," the palm faces away from the body.

Sentence Construction

In ASL, *to be* verbs are not used. As you saw in the phrase "My name is . . ." (page 133), you sign **MY NAME** and then fingerspell your name.

When putting together phrases with the signs you've learned, you will drop the words *am*, *is*, *are*, *was*, and *were*. Rarely will you sign the words *be*, *being*, and *become*. While this may feel foreign to you at first, make every effort to drop these words. You will sign the topic first and the describing word, whether adjective or verb, afterward.

For instance, if you wanted to say "I am happy," you would sign **I** (page 21) **HAPPY** (page 43). If you wanted to ask your child "Are you sad?" you would sign **SAD** (page 44) **YOU** (page 40) with your eyebrows raised to indicate a yes-or-no question.

To negate a sign or phrase, you can sign **NO** (page 28), but an easier way is to merely shake your head while signing the sign you want to negate. It's important that your facial expressions match. You can furrow your brow, purse your lips, or merely look unhappy.

For instance, if you wanted to say "I'm not happy," you would sign **I HAPPY** and shake your head and look unhappy while signing **HAPPY**. If you wanted to say "I'm not hungry," you would sign **I HUNGRY** (page 128) and, again, shake your head while signing **HUNGRY**.

Good

With both hands in a flat handshape, place the tips of the fingers of the dominant hand on your chin. Bring the hand down to land on the palm of the nondominant hand, which is facing up.

✳ **Memory Tip**

This sign is similar to **THANK YOU** (page 122), which can remind you that you're thanking someone for doing something good.

🧩 **Similar Sign**

This sign is often confused with **THANK YOU**. **THANK YOU** is done with one hand that ends at a 45-degree angle in front of the body, whereas **GOOD** ends with the palm facing up in the palm of the nondominant hand.

💡 **Teaching Tip**

Throughout the day, remark on your child's behavior and accomplishments by signing **GOOD** each time. You can do the same thing with other members of your family and friends who come by. Take the time to point out behaviors you want repeated, and sign **GOOD** to reinforce the meaning and the desired outcome.

Make it a game to find things that are good around the house, the neighborhood, or while running errands. They could include something that tastes good (candy, food at a favorite restaurant, etc.), someone smiling and being kind, a pretty drawing someone made, a person picking up toys, and anything else you can think of. Be silly, have fun, and call the game "Good Day." The goal of the day is to find as many good things as you can. The more varied, the better.

Bad

With both hands in a flat handshape, place the tips of the fingers of the dominant hand on your chin. Bring the hand down to land on the palm of the nondominant hand, but as it is brought down, twist the hand to be palm to palm, as if to clap. The dominant hand's palm ends facing down.

✳ Memory Tip

You turn the hand down to turn the behavior away from you.

🧩 Similar Sign

BAD is a twist on **GOOD** (page 142), just as **DON'T LIKE** (page 125) is a twist on **LIKE** (page 124). This is very close to the sign for **GOOD**, but you flip your palm so it is facedown instead of faceup. This is most often confused when someone is signing to you rather than when you sign it yourself.

💡 Teaching Tip

Look through your favorite storybooks and find instances of when a character makes a bad choice or when something bad happens. Sign **BAD** for each instance. Be careful what behaviors or ideas you tie this sign to, and be sure to point to the result, for instance, a broken window, rather than the person who broke it. This would also be a good time to point out the correcting behavior (apologizing or fixing the window) and signing **GOOD**. Don't dwell on this concept as much as you do for **GOOD**, unless your child has trouble understanding.

Sign Practice

INTRODUCTIONS

In the Deaf community, introductions are a large part of the culture. The introductions are much longer and more involved than they are in the hearing world. People in the hearing world are typically satisfied with learning only the person's name, but in the Deaf community, people want a lot more details and will soon know your life story.

It's important to practice your introductions. Here is what you should sign in your introduction:

HI YOUR NAME WHAT?

MY NAME . . .

I HEARING/DEAF/AUTISTIC.

I OLD . . .

To sign your age, you sign **OLD**, which is done with your dominant hand in the **O** handshape, held at the bottom of the chin. You pull your hand down, as if showing your long goatee, and close your hand in an **S** handshape. After you sign **OLD**, sign the number of your age (chapter 8, page 150).

INTRODUCTION FUN

Now let's practice introductions with a twist. Line up your kid's favorite stuffed animals and toys, and practice introducing yourself to each animal and toy. You can then introduce yourself to the toy and have your child pretend to be the toy that's introducing itself back.

After you have introduced yourselves, practice asking the toys questions. For instance, are they hungry? Do they like grapes? Are they sad? Ask as many questions as you can make up using the various signs in the book.

Remember, to ask a yes-or-no question using just one sign, simply raise your eyebrows and tilt your head forward. You can add to these questions by adding the sign **YOU** at the end. For instance, to sign **HUNGRY YOU?** just raise your eyebrows while signing both signs.

To ask if they like something, such as an apple, you can sign **APPLE LIKE YOU?** filling in whatever object or action you're wanting to ask about. Sign **JUMP LIKE YOU?** to ask, "Do you like to jump?"

If you use one of the wh-question signs—**HOW** (page 129) or **WHAT** (page 130)—be sure to furrow your eyebrows rather than raise them. **JUMP HOW** is one example.

After you've introduced yourselves to each toy and stuffed animal, have fun thinking of silly questions to ask.

PRACTICING EMOTIONS

As you know, when negating a sign, it's important to show negative facial expressions when signing. You can do this in a variety of ways. Do this in the way that feels most natural to you, the way you naturally express negativity. Common negative expressions are furrowed brows, pursed lips, squinting eyes, curled lip, scrunched nose, clenched teeth, or cocked eyebrow.

In ASL, you express many emotions with your facial expressions. Excitement, nervousness, surprise, terror, and confusion are a few you would show when signing. No one will know what you're thinking and feeling while you're signing if you aren't showing your emotions at the same time.

Use the emotion popsicle sticks from chapter 3 (page 53), and think of five different signs or phrases to sign together. Sign each of them with a neutral facial expression. Then pull out a random popsicle stick face and sign the same signs or phrases with the emotion of the popsicle stick.

For instance, if you were signing JUMP (page 115) and you pulled out the "angry"

popsicle stick, make your face look angry while signing JUMP. If you want to really show your anger, try changing the way your sign is "jumping" to show anger, as well.

Do this with each popsicle stick face and each sign that you've picked. Have fun, laugh, and get comfortable using your emotions to add to your signing.

Signing various signs while demonstrating anger or sadness may feel weird, but it's a very important grammar practice. When you are speaking, you show various emotions with your voice with inflection, volume, speed, and emphasis. In ASL, you do the same thing with the way you sign a specific sign and your face.

This exercise will help you feel more comfortable expressing various thoughts and feelings while you are signing, a vital aspect of ASL. You may never sign JUMP while being angry, but you and your child will develop the ability to express yourselves fully to others. ASL isn't a shortcut or abbreviated way to communicate; it's full and robust. Using facial expressions is one of the most effective ways to sign your complete meaning rather than just the surface meaning.

⑧

Alphabet and Numbers

THE ALPHABET IS vital to learn not only for fingerspelling but also to truly understand the handshapes that form the multitude of signs you will learn. Most of the signs use a variation of a letter or number in the shape they form. Get comfortable with the shapes of the letters, what they look like, and how to make them.

Letters are also essential for fingerspelling. Fingerspelling is a skill you will use in every signed conversation. Children can learn to fingerspell and recognize fingerspelling even if they don't know how to read. It's incredible! You don't need to push this from the start; instead, spend the majority of your time learning the signs. Once you feel comfortable with them, begin to introduce the letters and numbers, and practice them regularly and often. Use them often, as well.

Numbers can be tricky, so pay special attention to how they're formed and which way they face. Take your time to learn them and master them. Even when you're around hearing folks who use the traditional way of showing numbers, always use your ASL numbers. For instance, when hearing people show the number 3, it looks like the signing for the letter **w**. In ASL, **3** is signed with the middle finger, index finger, and thumb extended and the palm facing the body. Don't allow others to correct your child's hand; instead, explain that this is how it is signed, and show them the sign. They don't have to use it, but they should no longer correct your child.

Alphabet

There are four letters in the alphabet that are not signed with the palm facing outward. G and H are signed with the fingers pointed to the side and the palm facing the body. P and Q are signed with both the fingers and palm down. The rest of the letters are all signed with the palm facing the person you're signing with.

The most common letters to be signed incorrectly, with the palms facing the wrong direction, are C, D, F, O, P, and K. To sign these six letters correctly, keep your palm facing forward. They are pictured turned to the side only for clarity.

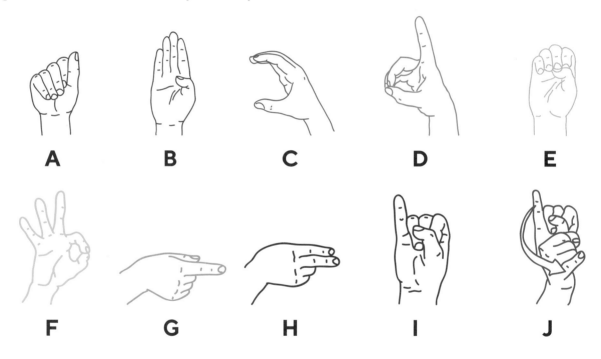

A B C D E

F G H I J

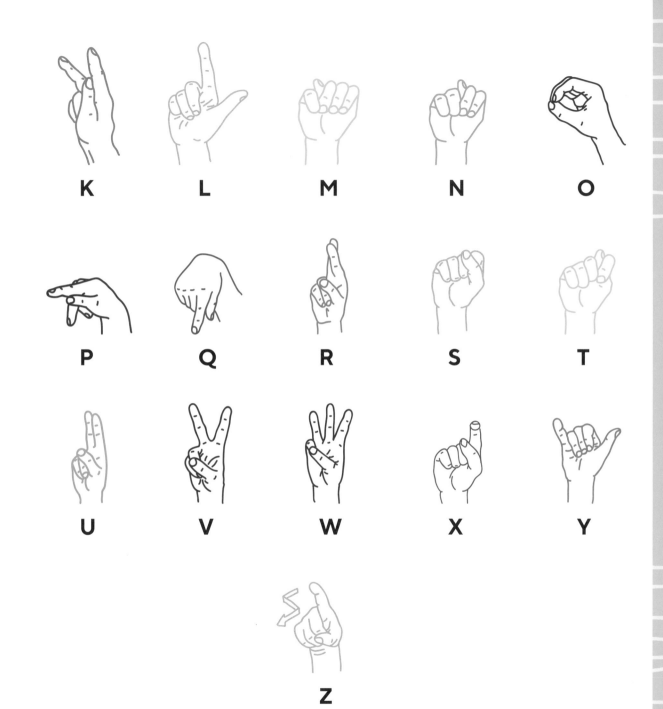

K L M N O

P Q R S T

U V W X Y

Z

Numbers

ASL numbers are all done with one hand. It's a very convenient way to count, as you'll soon see. Numbers 1 through 5 and 11 through 15 are signed with the palm facing your body. The rest of the numbers are signed with the palm facing away from the body.

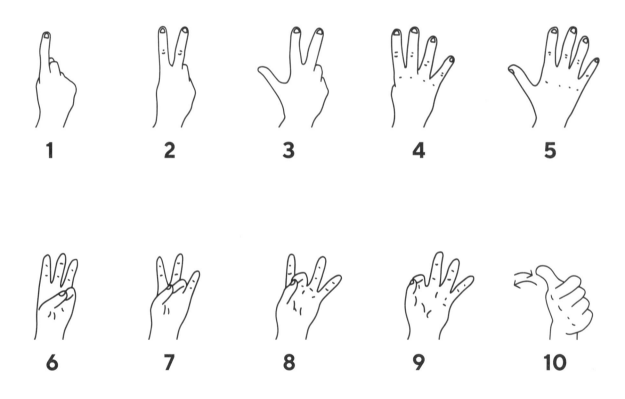

1   2   3   4   5

6   7   8   9   10

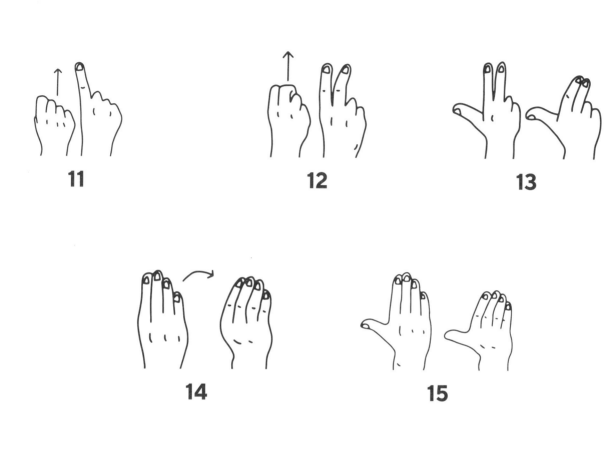

11

12

13

14

15

16

17

18

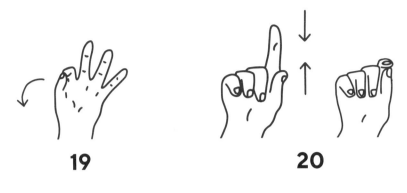

19

20

21

22

23

24

25

26 **27** **28**

29 **30**

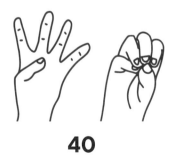
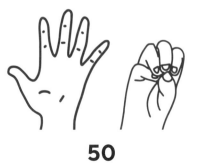
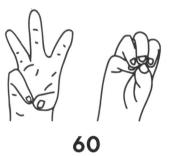

40 **50** **60**

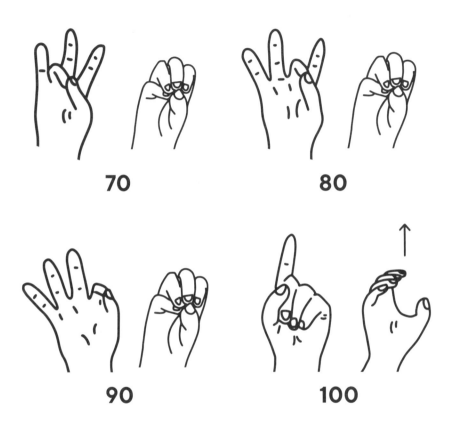

70

80

90

100

Sign Practice

SIGN A STORY: NUMBERS

To learn numbers 1 through 10, which is all your child will need to know at first, gather up your favorite number books and counting books. Each time they show a number, or have you count it, use your ASL numbers to count rather than the traditional way. Here are some excellent books to check out at the library to get you started:

Chicka Chicka 1, 2, 3 by Bill Martin Jr.; Ten Little Fish by Audrey Wood; Ten Apples Up on Top! by Dr. Seuss; and Five Little Monkeys Jumping on the Bed by Eileen Christelow.

COUNTING

You can practice counting objects and counting with ASL numbers with these two simple activities.

BEAN COUNTING

You'll need any type of dried bean and some small containers. Label each container with a number. If your child is quite young, start with 1 through 5, and as they get older, move to 1 through 10 and 1 through 20. Show them how to count with ASL numbers. Have them sign the numbers for each container. Then have your child count out the number of beans and put them in the right container. For example, if they are filling the number 4 cup, have them sign 1, 2, 3, and 4 before they drop in each bean.

PIPE CLEANER COUNTER

You'll need thick pipe cleaners and bright beads. It's easier for younger children to have bigger wooden beads to work with. Supervise them so they don't accidentally swallow a bead.

Write the numbers 1 through 10 on a piece of paper, and cut them out. Have your child choose a random piece of paper from the pile and help them or guide them as they put the number of beads on their pipe cleaner that corresponds to the number they chose. It may be easier for little hands to have one end of the pipe cleaner stuck into a ball of Play-Doh for stability. After they put the beads on the pipe cleaner, have them count the beads using their ASL numbers.

SIGN A STORY: THE ALPHABET

There are a multitude of alphabet books to choose from to teach your child both the English and ASL alphabets. You will want to practice these together on a regular basis. You may tire of the books you already have, so here are some other alphabet books to find at your library to avoid book boredom.

Alphabeep by Debora Pearson, *Dr. Seuss's ABC* by Dr. Seuss, *Animalia* by Graeme Base, *Z is for Moose* by Kelly Bingham, *Chicka Chicka Boom Boom* by Bill Martin Jr. and John Archambault, *The Handmade Alphabet* by Laura Rankin, *Firefighters A to Z* by Chris L. Demarest, *Alphablock* by Christopher Franceschelli, *A Was Once an Apple Pie* by Edward Lear, and *I Spy Letters* by Jean Marzollo.

LETTER HUNT

Craft stores have sheets of puffy letter stickers. Find your favorite set, and stick the letters in fun places throughout your home or outside. Be sure to test that the sticker doesn't ruin any surfaces. Tell your child you're going on a letter hunt.

If you want, you can write all the letters on a piece of paper they can mark as they find the letters, or simply enjoy hunting for the letters.

Search for the letter stickers together, and when your child finds one, have them sign the letter in ASL. They may need to be prompted a few times. If they sign it incorrectly, be sure to help them sign it accurately before moving on to the next letter. If your sticker sheet has multiples of each letter, be sure to use them all and hunt until you find them all.

RESOURCES

SITES FOR LEARNING ASL AND RESOURCES FOR PARENTS

American Society for Deaf Children: deaf children.org

My Deaf Child: www.mydeafchild.org

National Association of the Deaf: www.nad.org

Gallaudet University: www.gallaudet.edu /asl-connect

Dawn Sign Press: www.dawnsign.com

ASL Rochelle: www.aslrochelle.com

Life Print University: www.lifeprint.com

APPS

The ASL App

ASL with Care Bears

My Smart Hands Baby Sign Language Dictionary

Signing Time ASL

ASL Tales

Marlee Signs

VL2 Storybook Apps

DEAF COMMUNITY

Google search for "Deaf coffee chat," "Deaf club," and "ASL club" in your city

Deaf expos

ASL Slam: www.aslslam.com

Your local Registry of Interpreters for the Deaf (RID) chapter

Local college or university may have an ASL club that knows of the Deaf community around you

Deaf Linx: www.deaflinx.com

ASL BOOKS AND DVDS

Moses Goes to . . . series by Isaac Millman

Dad and Me in the Morning by Patricia Lakin

Once Upon a Sign DVD series

American Sign Language Babies series by Tina Jo Breindel and Michael Carter

ASL FOR ASD

Dr. Mary Barbera: www.marybarbera.com

The Verbal Behavior Approach by Mary Barbera

National Autism Resources: www.nationalautism
resources.com

BOOKS MENTIONED IN THE PRACTICE ACTIVITIES

Goldilocks and the Three Bears

Families by Ann Morris

Families Are Different by Nina Pellegrini

An Alphabet Salad by Sarah L. Schuette

Chicks and Salsa by Aaron Reynolds

Dragons Love Tacos by Adam Rubin

Eating the Alphabet by Lois Ehlert

Please Take Me for a Walk by Susan Gal

Go, Bikes, Go! by Addie Boswell

Chicka Chicka 1, 2, 3 by Bill Martin Jr.

Ten Little Fish by Audrey Wood

Ten Apples Up on Top! by Dr. Seuss

Five Little Monkeys Jumping on the Bed by Eileen Christelow

Alphabeep by Debora Pearson

Dr. Seuss's ABC by Dr. Seuss

Animalia by Graeme Base

Z Is for Moose by Kelly Bingham

Chicka Chicka Boom Boom by Bill Martin Jr.

The Handmade Alphabet by Laura Rankin

Firefighters A to Z by Chris L. Demarest

Alphablock by Christopher Franceschelli

A Was Once an Apple Pie by Edward Lear

I Spy Letters by Jean Marzollo

INDEX

ACKNOWLEDGMENTS

How does one truly express her gratitude to the multitude of people it takes to write and create a book? First off, I wouldn't be here if it weren't for my mother's belief in me to learn sign language and providing me ample opportunities to study it, even at great personal sacrifice. Thank you to my crazy beautiful family who shared in my excitement and have supported me every step of the way. I'm grateful to my ASL students, past and current, for their infectious curiosity and love of this perfect language.

I could not have done this without the incredible and talented people of Callisto Media. Thank you for this amazing opportunity, the chance of a lifetime to work with a wonderful team. Thank you to Vanessa and my kind-hearted editor, Justin Hartung. Thank you with all my heart, and I can't wait to do it again.

ABOUT THE AUTHOR

ROCHELLE BARLOW first began to learn ASL as a very young child. She learned on her own for many years, then worked with private tutors in high school and studied Deaf education at Utah State University. She worked at the School for the Deaf and Blind in Ogden, Utah, and after college, she interpreted for various school systems. Rochelle began teaching ASL over 15 years ago, and she adored her work with Deaf children, children with autism, and those with Down syndrome and their families. She began to teach at her local community centers, in co-ops, and in private schools and classrooms before beginning her own business teaching ASL online at ASL Rochelle. Rochelle loves to read, write, and watch British murder mysteries. She is the mother of six incredible children and lives in southern Oregon.